LETTS CREATIVE NEEDLECRAFTS

APPLIQUÉ

·JANE · WALMSLEY·

LETTS CREATIVE NEEDLECRAFTS

APPLIQUÉ

JANE
WALMSLEY

For John, Paula and Tim

First published in 1992
by Charles Letts & Company Ltd
Letts of London House
Parkgate Road
London SW11 4NQ

Designed and produced by Rosemary Wilkinson
4 Lonsdale Square, London N1 1EN

Editor: Hilary More
Illustrator: Richard Draper
Designer: Patrick Knowles
Photographer: Mark Gatehouse

A CIP catalogue record for this book is available from the British
Library

ISBN 1 85238 342 9

Typeset by Fakenham Photosetting Ltd, Fakenham, Norfolk

Printed in Belgium

CONTENTS

A fine example of a nineteenth century Baltimore Bride quilt, made up of 25 blocks with sashing strips and an intricate appliqué border.

DESIGN: PAST AND PRESENT

Appliqué is the placing of formal motifs, arranged in a design, on a plain background fabric. This form of needlework has been practised in the home, in great houses and palaces, on religious vestments and furnishings and on military and crusader banners from the medieval period to the present day.

Appliqué can be made in a variety of materials, such as cotton, wool, linen, silk, felt, suede and leather. The motifs can be stitched in place invisibly or decoratively using a variety of threads and embroidery stitches.

Appliqué is possibly the earliest form of pieced work – the oldest known example being a ceremonial canopy made from dyed gazelle hide now in a Cairo museum. Appliqué can be used to strengthen woven fabric, to repair, to decorate and to conserve. Sound areas of precious and rare silk, satin, brocade, printed cotton and linen fabrics, as well as embroideries where the foundation fabric had worn or rotted, would be cut out and appliquéd, in a new design, to a background fabric.

The flowering, literally and metaphorically,

of the age of English domestic embroidery occurred in the mid 16th century when bed furnishings, including curtains, coverlets, valances and pillows would be worked in embroidery and appliqué. 'Slips' embroidered in tent stitch on linen canvas, were cut out following the outline of the motif and were then applied to rich velvet fabrics, the cut edges being finished with couched cords.

During the 16th and 17th centuries, brilliantly colourful, painted and printed cotton bed covers (or palampores) were imported from India. At first the exotic plant and animal designs were printed on a red ground, which was 'not to the European taste', embroidery designs were then sent to India with the request that these new designs should be printed on a white or cream ground. The rarity value of these Indian textiles was further enhanced by laws being passed at different times during the 17th and 18th centuries which attempted to prohibit the importation of cotton fabrics into England in order to protect the home linen and wool industries. In time the lady of the house with her sophisticated taste, leisure and a household to help would cut out motifs from the otherwise worn textile and appliqué them to a new background fabric. The shapes would first be stuck in place using a flour and water paste. Today we have a modern equivalent for this purpose – the iron-on bonding adhesive.

The motifs could be attached by turning the seam allowance in and invisibly stitching in place, or by placing the design flat on the background fabric and attaching with close herringbone or buttonhole stitch, matching the colour of the thread to the background fabric. This type of appliqué is also known as *Appliqué Perse*.

Historical appliquéd articles can also illustrate the changing fashions of printed textiles from Indian chintzes, Egyptian and Chinese-influenced designs through to the fabrics featuring types of architecture and exotic game birds.

Appliqué, being less time consuming and, therefore, less expensive was often seen as a substitute for embroidery. Conversely, appliqué can be embellished and enhanced by embroidery.

The appliqué motif could be used as a picture, on a block or as a central panel of a bedcover surrounded by a succession of borders of whole cloth, patchwork or more appliqué.

In Britain, the furnishings and bedcovers made from appliqué were not always quilted.

Needlework was taken to America by European settlers and the economic need for the reuse of any sound pieces of textiles, reinforced by England passing laws in the mid 17th century to protect its trade monopolies with America, meant that appliqué not only survived but flourished.

As well as the British influences, the design heritage of the German and Dutch immigrants, who settled in Pennsylvania, have been preserved in the strong, simple decorative motifs such as the Tulip and Pineapple block designs and in the use of vibrant oranges, reds, yellows and greens. An example of the Tulip block design is shown in the quilt opposite.

Other well-known forms of American appliqué are the Friendship and Album quilts where each block is made and signed by a different person. The finished quilt was presented to a departing friend or minister; the bible is a recurring motif.

Baltimore Quilts were made in or near Baltimore during the first half of the 19th century. These impressive quilts made from a series of blocks each with a complex design, such as a basket of flowers, bowl of fruit or cornucopia, were possibly commercially drawn, the designs could then be purchased to sew at home. The blocks could be stitched together or be separated by setting strips. Frequently an elaborate appliqué border would also be added. The Baltimore Bride quilt illustrated on page 10 has patchwork setting strips and an exuberant, flowing, rose bud and leaf border.

Woven cloth and, therefore, needlework was taken to Hawaii by the wives of missionaries. The Hawaiian people adapted their own symbolic fruit and flower motifs into intricate designs for appliqué quilts. These were usually made from two strongly contrasting colours only; the large, whole cloth, appliqué fabric was folded a number of times into a triangle, the bold design cut, the fabric opened out and then stitched to the background material.

As with other American appliqué, Hawaiian work is always quilted but in a characteristic manner: here the stitching follows the contour of the appliqué design, each line being worked about 1.5 cm (½ in) apart covering the whole quilt and giving a lovely wave effect.

Ancient Celtic designs and Shadow appliqué, which possibly has its roots in the 18th century European embroidered muslins influenced by Indian embroidery, have been adapted to appliqué and quilting.

In Britain, appliqué has been used to document the invasion of Normandy in 1944. The Overlord Embroidery is a series of linen backed panels depicting various scenes from the action, worked in diverse fabrics, including uniform and net materials, edged with cords and embellished with embroidery. In the Pump Room in Bath there is a beautiful appliqué panel detailing 1000 years of monarchy and the 'Longleat Tree' in Longleat

A simple tulip motif makes a striking appliqué image. This Pennsylvanian German quilt was made circa 1840/50. The tulips are yellow and red with green stems and the zigzag border is in a floral red fabric.

House is a delightful pictorial history of the house.

Exciting, imaginative appliqué is a greater challenge than geometric patchwork, requiring the designer to have a clear mental picture of the appearance of the finished work.

The following projects introduce many of these traditional forms of appliqué as well as modern interpretations using the sewing machine.

Appliqué is the placing of fabric shapes onto a background fabric, which, being visible, becomes part of the design.

FABRICS

Cotton
Finely woven dress-weight 100% cotton fabrics are the easiest fabrics with which to work. They handle well, taking a sharp fold and do not fray too easily. Cotton wears and launders well and can be found in a wide range of plains and patterns. Lightweight closely-woven 100% cotton glazed furnishing fabrics are also available in a wide range of lovely colours. Wash cotton fabrics and remove selvages before use.

Polyester-cotton blends
These mixtures do not work well as they do not crease or press flat. They can be very thin, springy and tend to fray easily.

Silk
Silk is a luxury fabric found in a vast palette of beautiful colours. It is not easy to use as it frays and must be carefully handled as it marks easily. Must be dry cleaned.

Wool
Wool comes in a variety of weights and can be used for appliqué but usually in large simple designs. Wool can also be felted, then the appliqué shapes are cut without seam allowances. Wool should be dry cleaned.

Leather, suede, plastic
Can all be used for appliqué. In common with felt, the shapes are cut without seam allowances.

WADDINGS

If the article is to be quilted there is a choice of padding.

Polyester wadding
Comes in various weights, 2 oz, 3 oz, 4 oz and some even thicker. For fine quilting 2 oz wadding stitches well, is easy to obtain, lightweight and washes well.

Silk wadding
Comes in various forms: as caps, that is a triangle of spun fibres which need teasing out into an even layer; by the metre (yard) in two different weights – in this form the silk fibres are sandwiched between two papery layers.

Cotton wadding
Can be found either bleached or unbleached, by the metre (yard), with slightly stiff papery surfaces.

NEEDLES FOR NEEDLEMARKING

Use a long, strong darning needle with the eye pushed into a cork to mark the fold line on the appliqué shapes. The cork will protect the hand as well as make it more comfortable to hold.

Safety warning: When not in use always lay the needle down flat and keep another cork on the pointed end.

NEEDLES FOR HAND SEWING

Betweens
Short needles with small eyes used for appliqué and quilting.

Sharps
Slightly longer needles with small eyes used for appliqué, general sewing and tacking.

Crewel
These needles are the same length as sharps, but with a longer eye. Used for embroidery they can also be used for sewing and tacking.

Chenille
These needles have rounded eyes, thick shanks and sharp points. Use them where fabric threads need to be eased apart without breaking. Used for punch stitch.

NEEDLES FOR MACHINE SEWING

It is essential that the machine needles are sharp and the correct size for the style of stitching and type of material to be sewn.

PINS

A plentiful supply of good quality fine pins is essential. Please keep only pins in the box – no elastic bands, paper clips, etc.

SCISSORS

Always invest in good quality scissors. For the fabrics you will need a good pair of dressmaking scissors and a pair of small, pointed scissors. Make sure that all scissors are kept sharp. Keep a separate pair for cutting paper and card.

Sewing threads

Hand sewn appliqué

One of the secrets of fine, hand sewn appliqué is to use cotton sewing threads which exactly match the colour of the fabrics being applied. Use silk thread when stitching silk.

Machine stitched appliqué

A number of threads are available for machine sewing, including shiny, matt and metallic threads. As the stitching is usually meant to be visible the colour of the threads becomes part of the design.

Beeswax

Coat the sewing thread in wax when hand sewing as it helps to stop wear on the thread and knotting. Use a thread no longer than 46 cm (18 in) when hand sewing.

Templates

Plastic sheet

Thin translucent plastic, which can be cut with scissors is available from some specialist suppliers.

Thin white card

This is readily bought from art and stationery shops. Avoid old cereal packets as they are usually waxed.

Paper

Graph paper

Use this to plan and make scale drawings and to draft full size designs.

Drawing paper

Use for sketching design ideas.

Tracing paper

The final designs are traced onto good quality tracing paper prior to transferring the complete design to the background fabric.

Pens

Fine, black permanent ink felt tip pens are used to draw the final designs onto tracing paper. They give a good, clear line and will not mark and spoil the fabric. These pens are available from art and office supply shops and used for overhead projectors and marking plastic.

Pencils

Use HB lead pencils for general design and sketching.

A light blue colouring pencil (or white for dark fabrics) is used to transfer the design to the background fabric. These are available singly from art and office supply shops. Always keep the points very sharp.

Other equipment

Thimble

If you do not already use a thimble, try to learn to as it is almost a necessity when quilting.

Fine glasspaper

Smoothing the fabric, right side down onto a sheet of glasspaper, will prevent the fabric from moving while drawing round templates.

Ruler

A standard 30 cm (12 in) metal ruler to be used in conjunction with a craft knife when cutting straight-edged templates.

Eraser

Use a good quality, large, soft eraser to remove pencil lines from drawings.

Protractor, compass and set square

These pieces of equipment are invaluable for drafting blocks and geometric templates.

Rotary cutter and cutting mat

These must be used in conjunction with one another. Extremely effective when cutting layers of fabric and for borders, etc. The cutting mat is self-healing so the surface remains smooth.

Sewing machine

For machine-stitched appliqué a swing-needle machine is necessary, so you can cover the raw edges with a satin stitch – a closely-worked zigzag stitch on a machine.

Bonding web

Fusible fabric adhesive with a paper backing, useful when preparing some forms of machine appliqué.

Cork or polystyrene tile or pinboard

Pin the fabrics that are to be applied to a board to help in assessing the colours in the project and to keep the shapes in their correct sequence.

DESIGNING, CUTTING AND STITCHING

The term 'appliqué' covers a very wide variety of methods and forms using, among others, woven fabrics, felt, leather, suede and metallic threads and cords.

The area covered by this book refers particularly to the application of cotton fabric shapes to fabric backgrounds using a variety of methods, sewn by hand or machine, relying on line and colour for impact.

COLOUR

As the background fabric is visible, its colour is an important factor in the overall appearance of the design. When selecting a colour scheme a range of light, medium and dark tones is required together with a small amount of an accent colour which lifts the design, adding a little spice! Plain and patterned fabrics can be used, the only 'rule' to remember is that the fabrics are used in an interesting way enhancing the design.

A very useful family of fabrics are those where the printed design is a darker shade of the base colour.

A great deal of appliqué is based on plant forms, whether very stylized, as in the American traditional blocks, or in a more realistic representation, so green will be an important colour. Ensure that a number of different shades of green are used to avoid heavy, uninteresting areas. Look carefully at the blue, grey and yellow greens that are all around us in our gardens and parks, as well as at all the colours in the flower beds.

CHOOSING THE FABRICS

Generally the best results are achieved by using fine dress-weight 100% cotton fabrics (see page 14).

Some furnishing fabrics can be used as long as they are woven from fine threads and are closely woven 100% cotton.

Silk (see page 14) can, of course, be used to produce really stunning luxury items but they will need to be dry cleaned.

Woollen fabrics (see also page 14) can be used for larger, simple designs, perhaps appliquéd with a hand embroidery stitch such as buttonhole stitch.

All possible fabric sales outlets have to be investigated. As the fabrics are acquired cut a length from each piece about 7.5 × 2.5 cm (3 × 1 in) and staple this to a 10 cm (4 in) square of the chosen background fabric. The free ends can be laid on any possible new acquisition to test how it will work with those already bought. I keep my appliqué fabrics in a long shallow basket, individually folded to the width of the basket and placed on end so that a wonderful colour scan is always on view. Collecting the fabrics for an appliqué project, particularly a large one, can be a lengthy process, but be patient and enjoy the hunt!

WASHING THE COTTON FABRICS

That exciting glowing collection of fabrics must be washed! Washing shrinks the fabrics, tests for colour fastness and removes any dressing, making the fabrics more malleable. Iron the fabrics carefully ensuring that the threads are in alignment. If glazed fabrics are used, some of the glaze may wash off but this will not matter as they have been purchased for their inherent qualities of colour and fine weave. Fabric suppliers usually specify that fabrics should be washed at low temperatures and that biological powders should not be used.

THE DESIGN PLAN

There are various styles of appliqué each of which requires a different design approach.

Traditional American appliqué blocks are stylized designs often made from larger shapes all cut with 6 mm (¼ in) seam allowance. As is the case with all American pieced work, appliqué is intended to be quilted, so after each piece is stitched in place, the background fabric is cut away from the back of the shapes, leaving 6 mm (¼ in) turnings (diagram 1). This enables the finished appliqué to be quilted more easily as it is then only stitched through the top fabric, wadding and backing. (Stems, however, being very narrow are excluded).

When applying more naturalistic

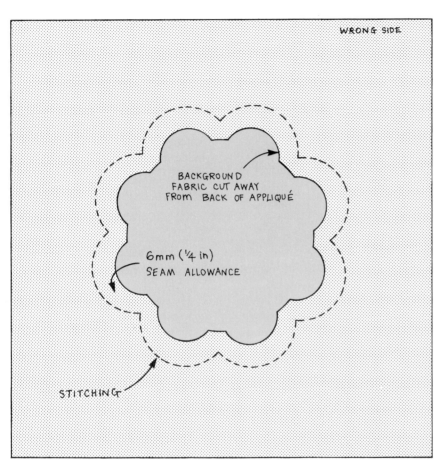

designs. See the Celtic cushion on page 47.

Hawaiian quilting
uses two strongly contrasting colours – the appliqué fabric is first folded and cut, then opened out and appliquéd onto the background fabric. Hawaiian work is always quilted in flowing lines of stitching, following the contour of the design. This can be seen on the cushion on page 59.

Fabric appliquéd with embroidery
using stitches such as buttonhole, herringbone, feather or punch stitch. An example is the tablecloth on page 63, which has a tulip motif appliquéd with punch stitch.

Reverse appliqué
is created when one or more fabrics are laid under the main colour which has been marked with the design. The top fabric is then progressively cut and stitched back revealing the fabric underneath. The scroll place mat is a good example, see page 75.

Shadow appliqué
is formed when coloured fabrics are cut to shape and laid on a foundation fabric, covered by a semi-sheer fabric and stitched in place, see the Sweet Pea panel on page 84.

Machine appliqué
Various methods are explored. In the Christmas cubes on page 51 the motifs are appliquéd from the front of the work, while in the Christmas

designs in which smaller, intricate shapes are overlapped, imitating the natural form, the background fabric is left intact. Quilting may also be used to outline the design and to enhance the appliqué, veins on leaves for example. Embroidery may also be used, for stamens, to shade petals, etc.

Other forms of appliqué where each has its own particular method of design, preparation and

construction are described with full instructions in the following projects.

Appliqué perse
where motifs are cut from printed fabrics and appliquéd in a new arrangement on a background fabric is shown on the child's pinafore, page 55.

Celtic appliqué
flattened tubes of bias-cut fabric are stitched into flowing, interwoven

hanging on page 79 the appliqué design is outlined from the back of the work then finished on the right side. The pictures also show a third method where the appliqué is three dimensional and detached.

Further American block designs are the Dresden plate, (shown on page 67) based on a circle, and Grandmother's Fan (page 40), where the appliqué motifs are based on a quarter circle.

Many of these forms of appliqué can, of course, be adapted to hand or machine stitching. When stitching by machine, satin stitch is commonly used so the effect of the stitching must be assessed. Should it match the fabric being applied or should it contrast? Should the stitching be as fine as possible or a really bold, wide outline? Should it be appliquéd by free machine embroidery? It is an exciting design area, so experiment and discover new ways of stitching.

Once the style of appliqué has been chosen it is necessary to make a scale plan, see page 23. Graph paper is a very useful aid in planning and drafting the designs. Even when more naturalistic elements are to be included it helps to evaluate the size and shapes of the area where the appliqué is to be worked. Once these have been determined, draw the full size background shape onto plain paper, then mark in the relevant appliqué design, full size within the given space.

TEMPLATES

Templates can be made from thin plastic or thin white card, depending on which method of preparation is to be used.

1 Trace the design shapes onto tracing paper, then glue onto the card. Number and transfer any marks relating to where the shapes overlap, etc.

2 Trace directly onto thin plastic sheets. Templates are cut to the finished size. Cut curved shapes with scissors. Cut straight-edged templates with a craft knife against a metal ruler. Lay the template plastic or card on a cutting board, place the metal ruler on the drawn template with its line exactly along the edge of the ruler. Stroking the knife down the ruler score the template line. This will ensure that the template is accurate. Continue running the knife along the scored line until the template is cut out (diagram 2).

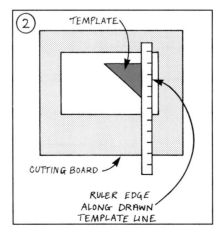

MARKING AND CUTTING FABRICS

Before using fabric, remove the selvages as they are made from inferior yarns. Smooth the fabric, right side down, onto fine sandpaper. This will hold the fabric preventing it from slipping. Turn the template over and place on the wrong side of the fabric.

Mark around the template with a well sharpened blue pencil, then transfer any positioning marks, overlaps, etc.

Cut out the shapes adding 6 mm (¼ in) seam allowances if making American blocks. Where naturalistic designs are to be sewn, add 3 mm (⅛ in) seam allowance.

Note: refer to each project for specific information regarding seam allowances and cutting details.

METHODS OF PREPARATION

Hawaiian, Celtic, shadow and machine appliqué all have their own particular method of preparation and construction so refer to the specific projects.

However, for American block designs and others, such as the Carnation picture, which are to be hand sewn, prepare the work using one of the following methods.

Needle marking
This is a method I have adapted from a traditional way of marking fabric for quilting. Push the eye end of a large, thick darning needle into

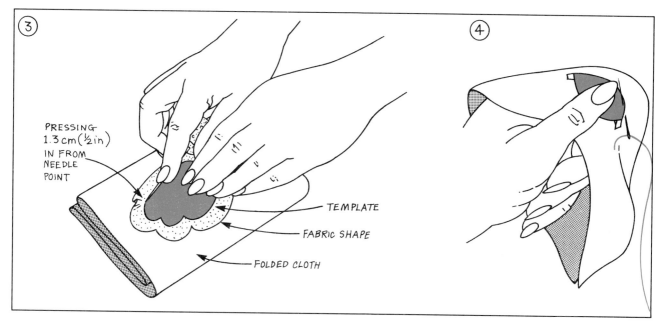

PRESSING
1.3 cm (½in)
IN FROM
NEEDLE
POINT

TEMPLATE

FABRIC SHAPE

FOLDED CLOTH

a cork. (*Always push a second cork over the pointed end when not in use.*) Make a pad from a folded smooth tea towel. Lay the fabric shape on the cloth pad, wrong side uppermost.

Needle mark along the template edge, keeping the cork and the needle under the hand and press on the needle about 1.3 cm (½ in) from the point of the needle (diagram 3). Turn the fabric to the right side: a sharp line will be apparent.

Tack around the shape on the right side, folding the seam allowance to the wrong side along the marked line, clipping into inner curves almost to the fold line as necessary. Where the fabric is very dark or heavily patterned it may be advisable to draw around the fold

line on the right side also, using a light-coloured pencil before tacking.

Where shapes are to be overlapped, needle mark the complete shape, but do not turn in the seam allowance in the areas which will be overlapped. The tacked shape may look very strange, but do not be tempted to press it with an iron at this stage as this would fix any line deviations and make it very difficult to mould the edge.

This method of marking is particularly useful when using very small shapes. It must be understood that appliqué is a marriage of marking, tacking, stitching and moulding. Thus, the folded edge is sculpted using the needle against the thumb as sewing progresses (diagram 4), and the final shape is

not determined until the stitching is finished.

Spray starch method
A small travel iron is ideal for this process. Cut the templates in white card. Cut out the fabric shapes with 6 mm (¼ in) allowance. Turn the template over and place centrally on the wrong side of the fabric shape. Clip into the inner curves almost to the stitching line.

Leaving the template in position, fold the seam allowance back over the template, press with the iron having first dampened the seam allowance with spray starch as follows. Spray the starch into the lid of the can and use the fingers to apply the starch to the seam allowances. When dry, remove the template and trim the seam allowances a little but do not cut off any tails that will form on sharp points (diagram 5).

TRANSFERRING THE DESIGN TO THE BACKGROUND FABRIC

Drawing the complete design onto the background fabric enables all the component parts to be correctly registered.

Draw the complete design with a fine permanent black felt tip pen on tracing paper. Place a white sheet of paper onto a flat surface, lay the tracing on top and hold in position with masking tape. Centre the background fabric over the design, tape down and trace the design onto the fabric with a blue pencil. If the background fabric is too dark to see traced lines, use a light box or tape the tracing and the background fabric to a strong light source, such as a window.

STITCHING ORDER

Work out the stitching sequence, so that relevant shapes overlap one another logically rather than trying to butt two folded edges together, see page 31 for an example on the Rose of Sharon design 1.

METHOD OF HAND STITCHING

First ensure that the colour of the thread exactly matches the fabric being applied and use a small fine needle. The blind stitching needs to be very small, tight and neat with evenly-spaced stitches.

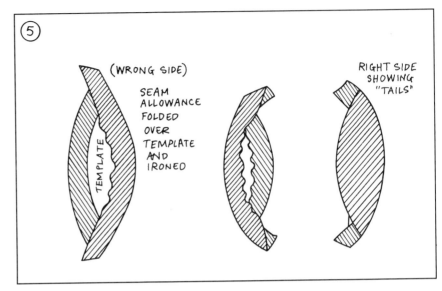

Begin by making a back stitch under the shape. Take a very small amount of the background fabric, bring the needle up and angle it so that a small amount of the under seam allowance is taken, bringing the needle out through the fold, go back into the background and so on. The thumbnail is firmly held just behind the fold and the needle is used to mould the edges, smoothing out any unwanted points and angles.

When stitching sharp outward points the tail is stroked in firmly with the needle. Where inward points and angles occur a neat semi-circle of overstitches is used to strengthen the area.

The stitching on the front will hardly be seen, however the stitches on the wrong side of the appliqué will be angled (diagram 6).

Remember – when sewing appliqué, the work is being handled and it may become rather creased, the tacked shapes may look extremely odd before they are stitched in place, but keep going, have faith, it will work!

When the appliqué is finished, press the work carefully on the wrong side.

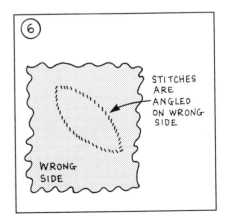

QUILTING

PREPARATION

Complete the appliqué top including any borders, press carefully from the wrong side.

Fold the backing fabric, which should be 5 cm (2 in) larger than the top fabric, into quarters, marking centre top, sides and bottom with glass-headed pins (diagram 7). Lay out on a flat surface wrong side uppermost, pin or tape down at the edges.

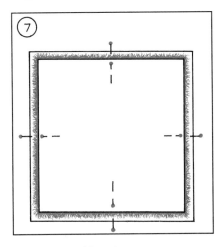

Fold the wadding into quarters, place on the top left-hand corner of the backing aligning the folds with marker pins on the backing. Open out carefully.

Fold appliqué into quarters right side in and mark with pins as before. Lay on top left quarter of wadding over backing, matching pins. Open out carefully. Pin the layers together from the centre, while gently smoothing the layers towards the outer edges.

TACKING

Tacking is the key to successful quilting. Tack even the smallest project very thoroughly. Use straight tacking stitches in the

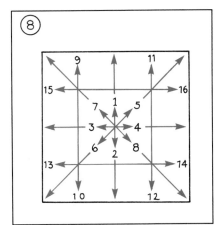

sequence shown (diagram 8). The lines of the tacked grid should not be more than 10 cm (4 in) apart and the lines of tacking worked around the outer edges should be small and firm.

FRAMES

A frame is not essential to hand quilting, but large round hoops can be used to quilt items as large as a bed quilt. Place the inner ring under the centre of the tacked quilt and secure with the top ring making sure that there is a little give in the textile to allow for manipulation when quilting. Quilt from the centre outwards, moving the hoop as necessary. Always remove the top ring at the end of each working session to allow the fabric to relax.

QUILTING STITCH

Cut a 46 cm (18 in) length of thread and use in a quilting needle (see page 14). Tie a neat knot and run the thread through beeswax to help prevent it from knotting. Insert the needle through the top fabric 2.5 cm (1 in) in front of where you will begin and run back through the wadding bringing the needle up at the starting point. Pull the thread until the knot is against the top fabric and pop it through into the wadding. Quilt through all three layers with running stitches. Keep the length of the stitch and the interval between the same length.

To finish the thread, make a knot near the fabric surface, slide the needle through the top close to the last stitch and into the wadding coming back up through the top about 2.5 cm (1 in) ahead. Pop the knot through into the wadding. Cut the thread close to the fabric surface. It will disappear into the wadding.

Note: It has been stated that quilting is a running stitch, but when quilting appliqué it may be necessary to stab stitch occasionally through the extra layers made by seam allowances.

When quilting round appliqué, stitch around the outline close to the stitching lines, adding further details and background stitching as desired.

AMERICAN APPLIQUÉ SAMPLER

Appliqué quilts are often made using traditional North American blocks. These hand stitched individual units of design can repeat the same motifs or, as in this sampler quilt, use different patterns for each block.

Traditional American blocks often feature stylized flowers and foliage where the design is quartered such as Rose of Sharon, designs 1 and 2, or designs where the two halves of the block are mirror images of one another, as in Heart of Leaves (see design sheet, page 28). The dimensions of the blocks used in any one quilt can vary, the size of a block required in a cot or child's bed quilt would be smaller than that required for a single or double bed. Another consideration must also be the complexity of the appliqué block – a simple design will fit successfully into a smaller area.

Plan the design carefully. First choose the block or blocks you wish to use, then take accurate measurements to determine the size of the finished article. From these measurements it will be possible to assess the size of the individual blocks and borders. For a single or double bed quilt, a block could measure from 30 cm (12 in) to 46 cm (18 in) square.

Now you must decide on how the blocks should be repeated over the quilt: will they be worked in every square, on point or alternated with plain fabric squares? Another decision is whether to use appliqué on its own or to include panels and borders of fabric or patchwork.

See the planning sheets on pages 26 and 27, which mainly feature the Rose of Sharon design 1, for just a few of the ways the blocks can be used.

Draw the overall size of the quilt, to scale, on graph paper. This will help the planning process as the size and shape of the areas to be appliquéd, as well as the borders, are determined.

DRAFTING THE BLOCKS

Draw the full finished size of the block on graph paper. Divide the area into quarters, then draw across the square diagonally to divide it into eighths, thus dividing the block into eight right-angle triangles. Many of the designs including the Rose of Sharon shown, can be divided into these eight sections.

Lightly sketch the complete design onto the divided square. One of these sections will look more pleasing than the rest, this will be the master. Draw over this section with black felt tip pen. Erase all sketch lines from the sections. Trace the master section onto tracing paper using felt tip pen, including the quarter and diagonal lines.

Match the master tracing over the division lines on the graph paper and tape securely in place. Slip a

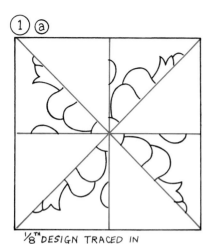

1/8 TH DESIGN TRACED IN
ALTERNATE SECTIONS

DESIGN TURNED
OVER AND TRACED

piece of carbon paper underneath and draw around the design with a sharp-pointed pencil. Repeat in the other three alternate triangles (diagram 1a).

Turn the tracing over and draw in the remaining sections completing the design (diagram 1b).

If the design divides down the middle as in Heart of Leaves, trace one half of the design then turn over the tracing to complete the design.

Martha Washington's Wreath and other circular based designs are drafted in a slightly different way. After the block has been divided into eighths use compasses to draw the circle, i.e. the stems. Draw a single flower in the desired position. Trace off three flowers and glue each one in its correct position. The leaves are evenly spaced around the block.

Cut out the templates and fabrics and prepare for stitching as detailed in the Skill File, page 18.

If the appliqué is to be quilted, the backing fabric is cut away from each shape after it is sewn in place, leaving 6 mm (1/4 in) seam allowances (excepting the stems). This means that there will only be one layer of top fabric, wadding and backing fabric to be quilted, allowing for finer, easier stitching.

In the quilt shown there are four traditional blocks set square – Martha Washington's Wreath, Rose of Sharon (design 1), Rose of Sharon (design 2) and Heart of Leaves. The finished size of each block is 31.5 cm (12½ in).

To create a more interesting effect, a variety of cotton fabrics in pinks and greens on an ivory background have been used in the quilt. It was

finished with simple fabric borders cut in two different widths. Templates and stitching sequences for the blocks are given on pages 30 to 39.

ASSEMBLING THE APPLIQUÉ BLOCKS

The blocks can be stitched by hand or by machine.

First press each block carefully on the wrong side gently pulling it back into shape.

A seam allowance of 1.3 cm (½ in) is added to the background fabric (instead of the usual 6 mm (¼ in) to allow for the fabric fraying while the block is stitched.

The finished blocks must all be the same size. When each block is completed, measure and mark half the block size on each side of the

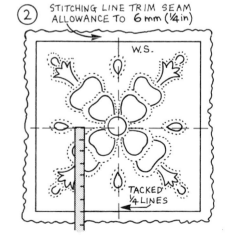

② STITCHING LINE TRIM SEAM
ALLOWANCE TO 6 mm (¼ in)

W.S.

TACKED
¼ LINES

tacked horizontal and vertical centre lines. Use a blue pencil and ruler to join up the marks, this will be the finished size of the block (diagram 2). Trim the seam allowance beyond these marks to 6 mm (¼ in).

Note: It is always easier to stitch in straight lines. Blocks set on point are stitched together in diagonal strips.

SETTING (OR SASHING)

Mark and cut the horizontal strips to the desired width and finished length of the block, plus 6 mm (¼ in) seam allowance all around. Place the block and setting strip with right sides together: pin, matching centres and ends of stitching lines exactly. Stitch together, press the seam allowances onto the setting strip.

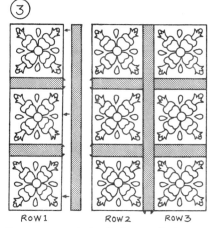

ROW 1   ROW 2   ROW 3

Repeat, to stitch all the vertical strips together in the same way (diagram 3, row 1).

Cut vertical strips to the desired width and finished length of the number of blocks *plus* the finished width of the horizontal setting

strips *plus* 6 mm (¼ in) seam allowance all around. Mark the points at which the horizontal setting strips will meet the vertical strips in the seam allowances on both edges. This will ensure that all the blocks and strips are in alignment.

Place the setting strip to the strip of block with right sides together; pin the matching marks on the vertical setting strip to the ends of the horizontal strips and in the centres of the blocks. Tack, then stitch together. Press seam allowances onto the long setting strips.

BORDERS

Measure the completed appliqué top both horizontally and vertically through the centres to establish the inner measurement of the border.

Cut the border strips to this measurement *plus* twice the width of the borders *plus* 6 mm (¼ in) all around. If two or more borders are to be used, cut the borders to required length and width and stitch together first into a single piece, pressing the seam allowances both the same way.

Mark the quilt top and border strips with pins (diagram 4). Lay the borders on the appliqué top with right sides together, matching pins. Tack and stitch on all four sides along the marked stitching lines only, not into the seam allowances on the outer edges of the appliqué top. Press seam allowances onto the

borders, leaving two overlapping border strips at each corner (diagram 4a).

Lay one corner of the appliqué top on a flat surface with the strips at right angles to one another. Take the top strip and fold it underneath at 45°, pivoting on the stitching point. Tack across the mitre that is formed; stitch and trim seam allowance (diagram 4b). Stitch all corners in the same way.

Quilt the appliqué if desired, see the Skill File page 21 and/or finishing suggestions.

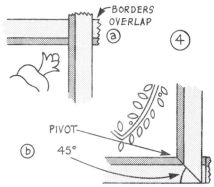

BORDERS OVERLAP

(a)

(4)

PIVOT

(b) 45°

PLANNING SHEET

① BLOCKS SET TOGETHER

② WITH SETTING STRIPS

③ WITH ALTERNATING PLAIN SQUARES

④ ALTERNATING BLOCKS (WHIG ROSE VARIATION)

PLANNING SHEET

⑤ BLOCKS SET ON POINT

⑥ SET ON POINT WITH SETTING STRIPS

⑦ HEART OF LEAVES

THE DESIGN IS PLACED ON A BACKGROUND SQUARE
SET ON POINT

⑧ SET ON POINT

ALTERNATED WITH PLAIN SQUARES AND TRIANGLES

ROSE OF SHARON (1)

ROSE OF SHARON (2)

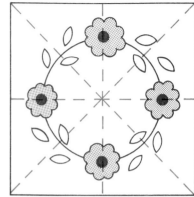

MARTHA WASHINGTON'S WREATH

HEART OF LEAVES

WHIG ROSE VARIATION

USED ALTERNATELY

OAK LEAF

DOTTED LINES
ON WHIG ROSE
SHOW QUILTING

SWAGS (BORDER)

TRAILING ROSE BUDS (BORDER)

MARTHA WASHINGTON'S WREATH

If the work is to be quilted, cut the background fabric away from the back of each appliqué flower and leaf as you stitch.

CUTTING DETAILS

(Makes one block)
Draw up the templates (page 30) and circle guide. Cut out the pieces, adding 6 mm (¼ in) seam allowance all around.
Template 1: 4 shapes
Template 2: 4 shapes
Template 3: 12 shapes
Template 4: 4 shapes
Cut one 34 cm (13½ in) square of fabric for background. Mark the quarter lines with coloured tacking stitches.

TRANSFERRING THE DESIGN

Open out the circle guide (page 30). Match the fold lines to the tacked quarter lines on the right side of the background fabric. Draw around the edge of the circle with blue pencil. Remove the circle.

Draw around flower template 1, positioned centrally over the tacked lines.

STITCHING SEQUENCE

(See also diagrams overleaf)
Fold each bias strip in half lengthwise and pin along the stem lines with the folded edge towards the centre. The ends start and finish under the flowers. Sew through all

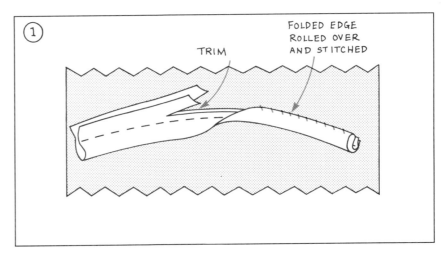

three layers with running stitch. Trim excess fabric, then roll the folded edge of the stem over the seam allowance and slipstitch in place (diagram 1).

Turn in the seam allowances and tack around each flower, clipping at inner points. Tack and stitch in place, covering the ends of the stems.

Run a gathering thread around the flower centre. Place the card circle template centrally on the wrong side of the fabric (diagram 2). Pull the gathering thread up tight and press (diagram 3). Carefully remove the card. Stitch the flower centre in place. Repeat with each centre.

Turn in the seam allowance around each leaf. Place the leaves evenly around the wreath as shown in the photograph; pin in place. Stitch the leaves in place, stroking in the tails which appear on the points with the needle as you stitch.

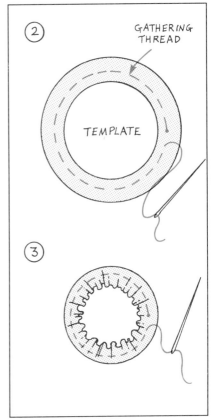

TEMPLATES

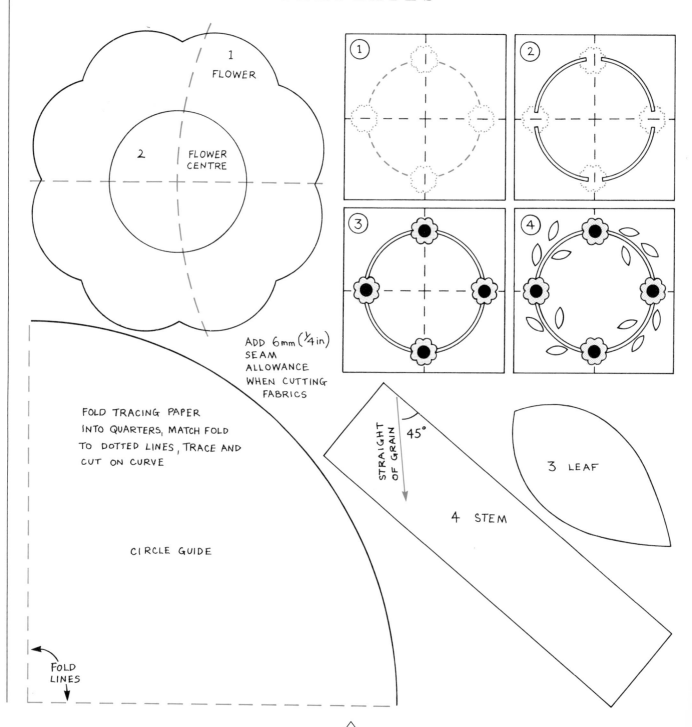

1 FLOWER

2 FLOWER CENTRE

ADD 6mm (¼in) SEAM ALLOWANCE WHEN CUTTING FABRICS

① ② ③ ④

FOLD TRACING PAPER INTO QUARTERS, MATCH FOLD TO DOTTED LINES, TRACE AND CUT ON CURVE

CIRCLE GUIDE

STRAIGHT OF GRAIN

45°

4 STEM

3 LEAF

FOLD LINES

ROSE OF SHARON
(design 1)

If the work is to be quilted, cut the background fabric away from the back of each appliqué flower and leaf as you stitch.

CUTTING DETAILS

(Makes one block)
Draw up templates (pages 32–3), the dotted lines indicate where each shape is overlapped. Make templates to the dotted lines and also add the marks. Make a quarter design outline guide in card.

Cut out the pieces adding 6 mm (¼ in) seam allowance all around.
Template 1: 4 shapes
Template 2: 4 shapes
Template 3: 4 shapes
Template 4: 4 shapes
Template 5: 1 shape
Template 6: 4 shapes
Add marks in seam allowances.

Cut one 34 cm (13½ in) square of fabric for background. Mark the quarter lines with coloured tacking.

TRANSFERRING THE DESIGN

On the right side of the fabric, carefully match the quarter design outline shape to the centre of the background fabric. Draw around it with blue pencil. Repeat to mark in all quarters, to complete the design.

STITCHING SEQUENCE

(See also diagrams above)
Turn in the outer edge of the bud

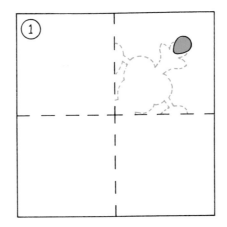
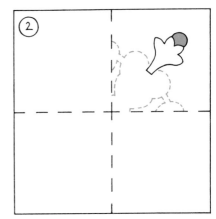
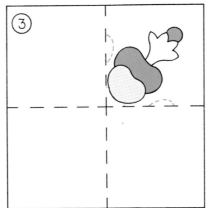
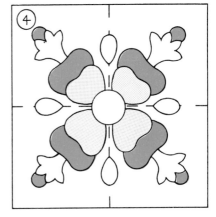

seam allowance from mark to mark. Pin in place and stitch to the background along the folded edge only.

Turn in the seam allowance all around the calyx except for the base. Pin and stitch in place overlapping the unstitched base of the bud.

Turn in the seam allowance of the outer petal from mark to mark. Pin and stitch, covering the base of the calyx along the folded edge.

Turn in the outer edge of the inner petal and stitch in place overlapping the base of the outer petal.

Repeat these steps for each quarter of the design.

Gather round the flower centre; pull up round the card circle template; press and stitch the centre in place as for Martha Washington's Wreath. Turn in the seam allowance on the leaves and stitch in position in the same way as for Martha Washington's Wreath.

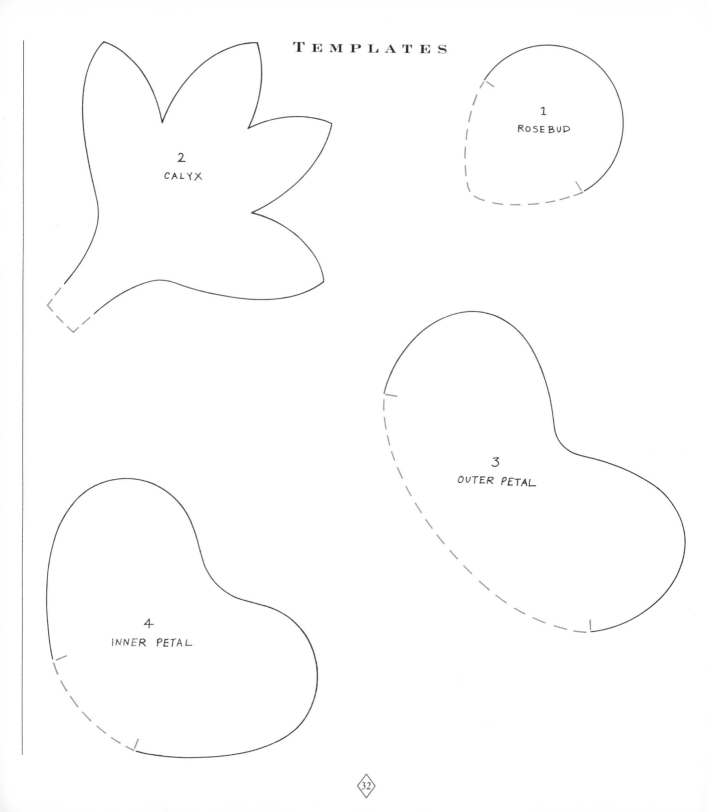

TEMPLATES

2
CALYX

1
ROSEBUD

3
OUTER PETAL

4
INNER PETAL

TEMPLATES

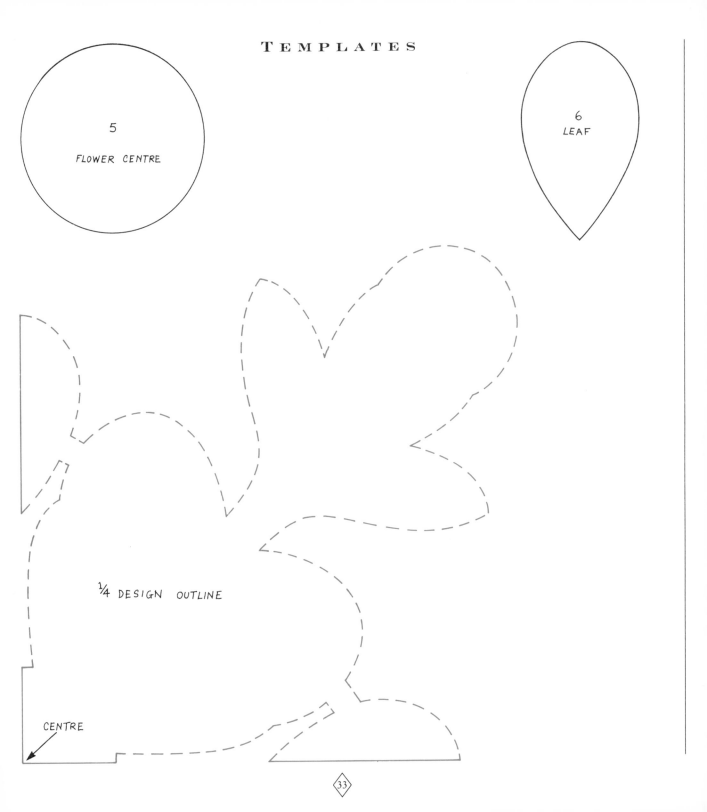

5

FLOWER CENTRE

6
LEAF

¼ DESIGN OUTLINE

CENTRE

ROSE OF SHARON
(design 2)

If the work is to be quilted cut the background fabric away from the back of each appliqué flower and leaf as you stitch.

CUTTING DETAILS

(Makes one block)
Draw up templates (pages 35–6). Make a quarter design outline guide. Cut out the pieces adding 6 mm (¼ in) seam allowance all around.
Template 1: 4 shapes
Template 1a: 4 shapes
Template 2: 4 shapes
Template 3: 4 shapes
Template 4: 8 shapes
Template 5: 1 shape
Template 6: 1 shape
Template 7: 1 shape
Add marks in seam allowances on buds.

Cut one 34 cm (13½ in) square of fabric for background. Mark the quarter lines with coloured tacking stitches.

TRANSFERRING THE DESIGN

On the right side of the fabric, match the quarter design to the centre of the background fabric. Draw around it with the blue pencil. Repeat in all quarters.

STITCHING SEQUENCE

(See also diagrams above)
Turn in the seam allowance around the pointed end of the bud from

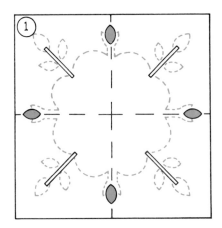
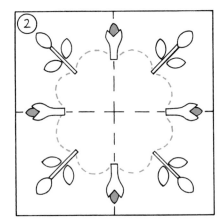

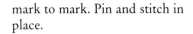

mark to mark. Pin and stitch in place.

Make the stems in the same way as for Martha Washington's Wreath.

Turn in the seam allowance all around calyx except the base. Pin and stitch in place.

Turn in the seam allowance around the four leaves (template 3). Pin and stitch the leaves in place covering the ends of the stems.

Turn in the seam allowance all

around the eight leaves (template 4) pin and stitch in place on either side of the stems.

Mark the quarter lines on the outer rose fabric. Turn in the seam allowance clipping to the inner curves. Match up the quarter lines on the rose to the quarter lines on the background fabric. Tack and stitch in place. Prepare and stitch the inner rose in the same way.

Turn in the seam allowance around the rose centre. Pin and stitch.

TEMPLATES

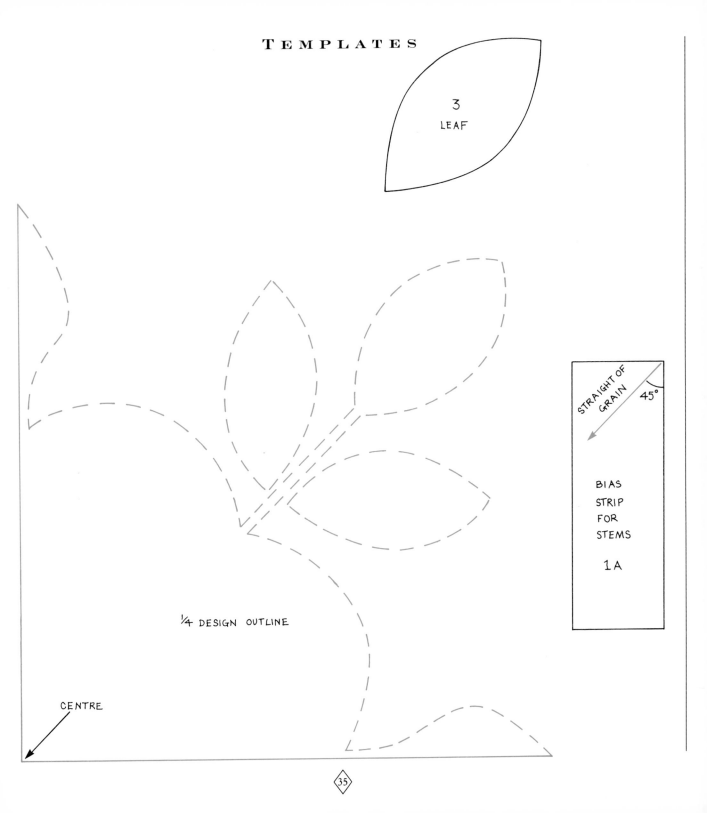

3
LEAF

STRAIGHT OF GRAIN

45°

BIAS
STRIP
FOR
STEMS

1 A

¼ DESIGN OUTLINE

CENTRE

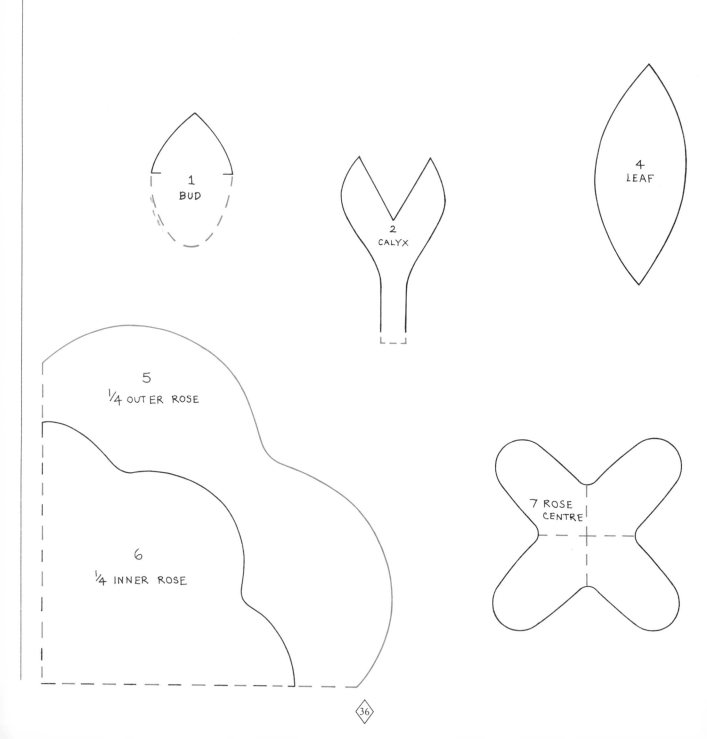

1
BUD

2
CALYX

4
LEAF

5
¼ OUTER ROSE

6
¼ INNER ROSE

7 ROSE
CENTRE

HEART OF LEAVES

If the work is to be quilted cut the background fabric away from the back of each appliqué leaf as you stitch.

CUTTING DETAILS

(*Makes one block*)
Draw up the templates (pages 38–9). Cut out each piece adding 6 mm (¼ in) seam allowance all around.
Template 1: 1 shape
Template 2: 3 shapes
Template 3: 40 shapes
Template 4 (× 2): 38 × 2.5 cm (15 × 1 in) cut on bias
Template 5: 10 shapes, without adding seam allowance.

Cut one 34 cm (13½ in) square of fabric for background. Mark quarter lines with coloured tacking stitches.

TRANSFERRING THE DESIGN

Draw centre horizontal and vertical lines on a sheet of tracing paper. Match the vertical and horizontal lines on the quarter designs illustrated to those on the tracing paper; trace half the design. Draw over the tracing with a black felt tip pen. Erase all pencil lines.

Tape the tracing to a flat surface. Slip white paper under it. Centre the background fabric, right side up over the tracing, matching quarter lines. Draw the half design onto the fabric with blue pencil. Lift off the

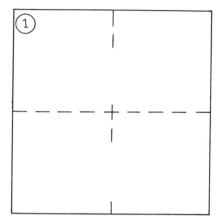

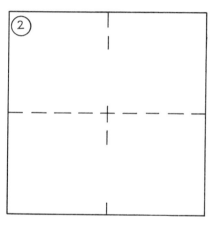

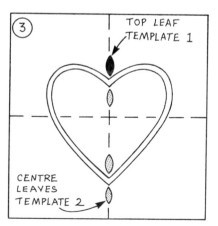

TOP LEAF TEMPLATE 1

CENTRE LEAVES TEMPLATE 2

fabric, remove the tracing. Turn the tracing over and tape down. Realign the background fabric over the tracing and draw in the left-hand side.

STITCHING SEQUENCE

(*See also diagrams left*)
Stitch the bias strips to the heart outline from centre top to lower centre point with the folded edge of the strip towards the centre of the heart, as shown in Martha Washington's Wreath, but in this case, neaten the ends.

Turn in the seam allowance on the leaf (template 1) and pin at top centre. Stitch in place, stroking in the tails with the needle as you stitch. Treat the three leaves made using template 2 in the same way, stitching in place at lower top and centre base.

Turn in the seam allowance on all other leaves made from template 3, stitching in position as shown.

Gather around each berry circle and pull up tight round a very small amount of wadding; secure with a backstitch (diagram 4). Hold firmly in position with raw edges against the background fabric. Sew securely with small, tight stitches.

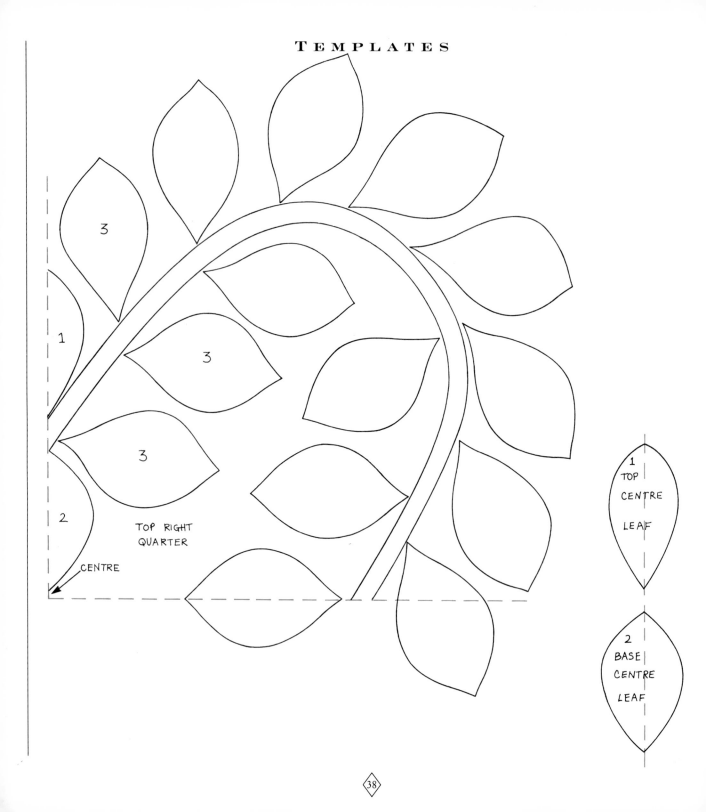

TEMPLATES

3

1

2

3

3

TOP RIGHT
QUARTER

CENTRE

1
TOP
CENTRE
LEAF

2
BASE
CENTRE
LEAF

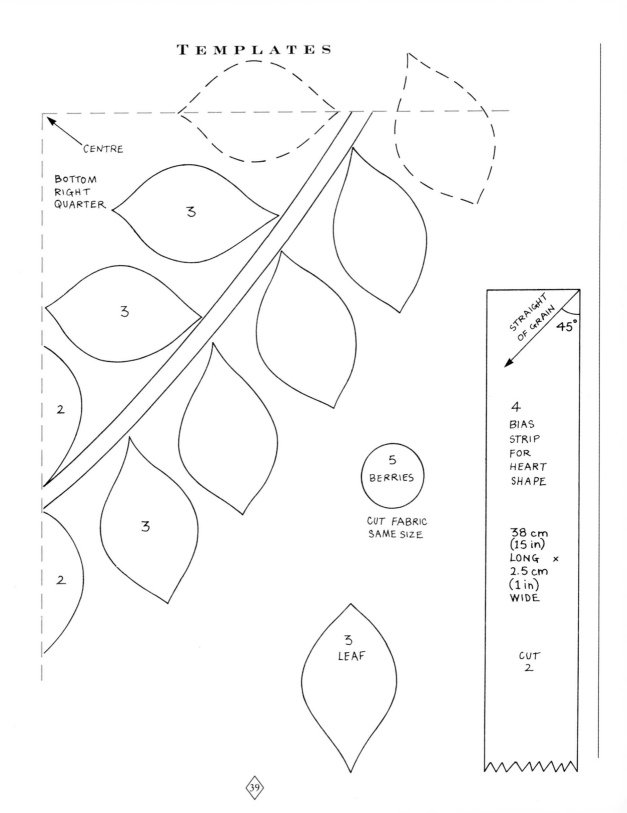

CENTRE

BOTTOM
RIGHT
QUARTER

3

3

2

3

2

5
BERRIES

CUT FABRIC
SAME SIZE

3
LEAF

STRAIGHT
OF GRAIN

45°

4
BIAS
STRIP
FOR
HEART
SHAPE

38 cm
(15 in)
LONG ×
2.5 cm
(1 in)
WIDE

CUT
2

FESTIVE APRON

Fan appliqués have been applied to both the bib and pocket of
this apron and the result would make a lovely present – try it in
different colours or fabrics that tie into the kitchen decor.
Create the apron in cotton fabrics for a crisp result
and easy-care features.

REQUIREMENTS

1.40 m (1½ yd) of 115 cm
(45 in) wide red cotton
fabric
30 cm (¼ yd) of 115 cm
(45 in) wide cotton
fabric, in colour A
30 cm (¼ yd) of 115 cm
(45 in) wide cotton
fabric, in colour B
30 cm (¼ yd) of 115 cm
(45 in) wide cotton
fabric, in colour C
30 cm (¼ yd) of 115 cm
(45 in) wide cotton
fabric, in colour D
Plastic sheet or thin card
for templates
HB pencil
Sharp craft knife, metal
ruler and cutting board

CUTTING DETAILS

Make templates for the appliqué
(pages 44–5) as described in the
Skill File, page 18, adding 6 mm
(¼ in) seam allowance all around.

Bib:
Template 1: 1 in colour A
Template 2: 1 in colour B
Template 3: 1 in colour C
**Template 4 (template 3
reversed):** 1 in colour A
**Template 5 (template 2
reversed):** 1 in colour B
**Template 6 (template 1
reversed):** 1 in colour C

Pocket:
As for bib, but to dotted lines on
templates

Bib and pocket:
Template 7: 2 in colour D

**From red cotton fabric cut
apron pieces:**
Apron skirt: 64 × 89 cm (25
× 35 in)
Bib backing: 23 cm (9 in) square
Bib edging: 23 × 7.5 cm (9 ×
3 in)
Pocket backing and facing: 2 ×
18 cm (7 in) squares
Side bib and neckband: 112 ×
7.5 cm (44 × 3 in); join as
necessary
Waistband and ties: 137 × 7.5 cm
(54 × 3 in); join as necessary

FINISHED SIZE

Approximately 86 cm (34 in) long
(without neck strap)

Working the appliqué

Pin out appliqué shapes for the bib and pocket in the correct sequence (diagram 1).

On the wrong side of the bib and pocket backing squares, draw a line diagonally from corner to corner. Mark the stitching lines around the squares 1.3 cm (½ in) from the outer edge. Mark the position of template 7 (diagram 2).

Pin the first shape (template 1), right side up in position on the backing (diagram 3). Pin the second shape over the first with right sides together. Stitch through all three layers and press this section upwards (diagram 4). Repeat until all the shapes are stitched in place, ensuring that the stitching line of the third section falls on the diagonal line marked on the backing.

Turn the curved edge of the ¼ circle to the wrong side, place on the backing over raw edges; slipstitch in place.

Making up

Place the bib edging along the appliqué bib top right sides together and stitch; turn over the raw edge, tuck under seam allowance and slipstitch over previous stitching (diagram 5).

Press 1.3 cm (½ in) to wrong side along one edge of the neckband. Stitch the opposite edge to either side of the bib, with edges level

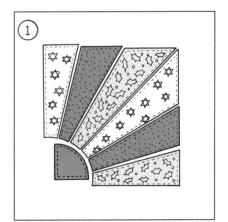

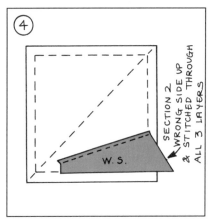

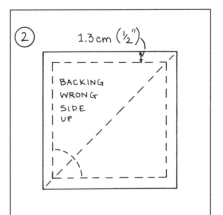

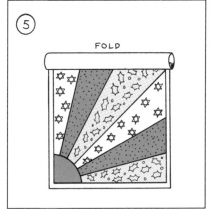

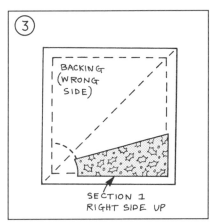

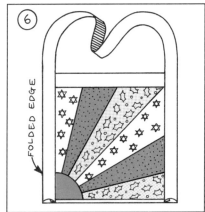

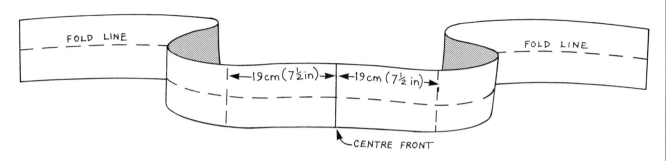

FOLD LINE

19cm (7½in)   19cm (7½in)

CENTRE FRONT

FOLD LINE

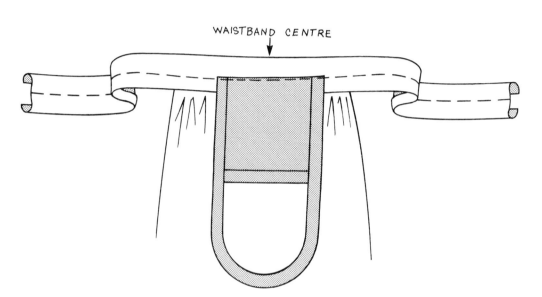

WAISTBAND CENTRE

with base edge of bib (diagram 6, on previous page). Press the band in half; stitch down the length.

Place the appliqué pocket and the backing right sides together; stitch all around, taking 1.3 cm (½ in) seam allowance and leaving opening centrally on one side. Trim the corners and turn to the right side; slipstitch across opening.

Hem both short and one long edge of the skirt. Mark the centre front.

Work two rows of gathering stitches across the top edge. Press the waistband in half lengthwise. Mark the centre and again 19 cm (7½ in) on either side of the centre front (diagram 7). Match the centre of the skirt to the centre of the waistband with right sides together. Match the outer marks to the edges of the skirt, pull up the gathers to fit. Stitch together between the gathering lines. Press the waistband away from the skirt.

Place the bib over the apron, matching centres. Stitch together through all thicknesses matching the bib stitching line to the fold line on the waistband (diagram 8). Neaten the lower edge of the bib. Fold the waistband to the back along the creased line; turn in 1.3 cm (½ in) turnings along the waistband, including the ends; stitch through all thicknesses. Place the pocket on the apron in desired position; topstitch in place.

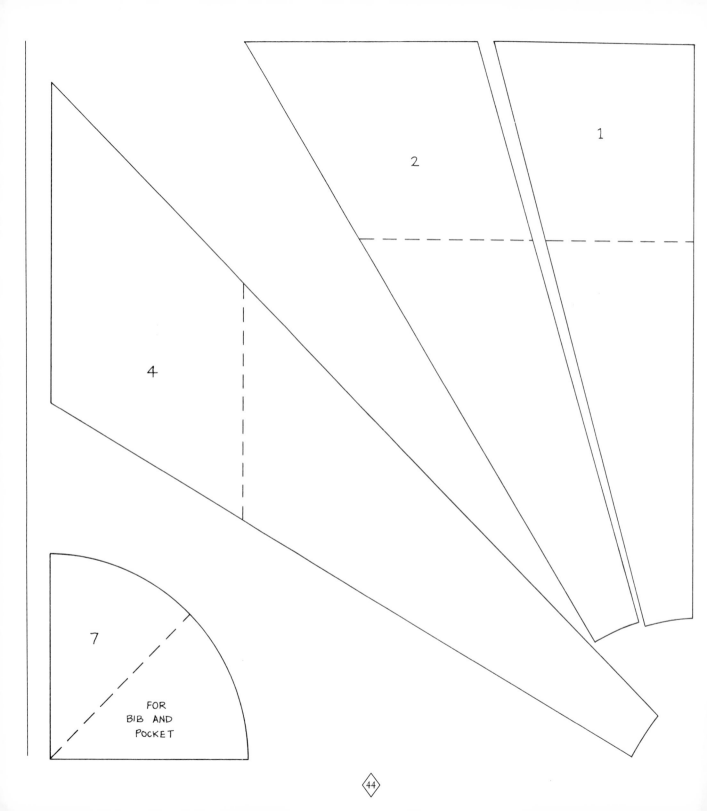

1

2

4

7

FOR
BIB AND
POCKET

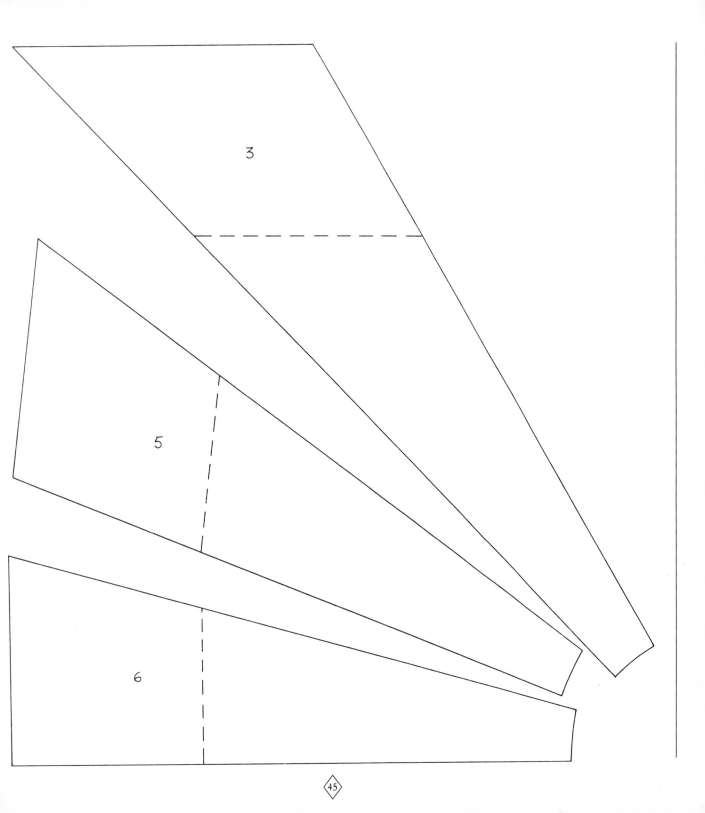

3

5

6

CELTIC CUSHION

The ancient art form of the Celts with its interlacing knotwork, twisted plaits and spirals has survived on carved stone and illuminated manuscripts. The Lindisfarne Gospels, the Book of Kells, and carved stonework in the North of England, Scotland and Ireland are famous examples. Here a motif has been adapted for a particular type of hand stitched appliqué.

REQUIREMENTS

1.40 m (1½ yd) of 115 cm (45 in) wide cream cotton fabric for background, backing and cushion backing

50 cm (½ yd) of 115 cm (45 in) wide dark red cotton fabric

50 cm (½ yd) of 115 cm (45 in) wide green cotton fabric

70 cm (¾ yd) of 115 cm (45 in) wide 2 oz wadding

Matching sewing threads

1 cm (⅜ in) Celtic gauge or three 1 cm (⅜ in) strips of white card

Tracing paper

Fine black permanent ink felt tip pen

Light blue pencil

46 cm (18 in) square cushion pad

CUTTING DETAILS

Cream fabric: Cut three 48.5 cm (19 in) squares.

Green and dark red fabrics: Cut sufficient 3.5 cm (1¼ in) wide bias strips (45° from selvage) for the appliqué strips.

FINISHED SIZE

Cushion measures 46 cm (18 in) square

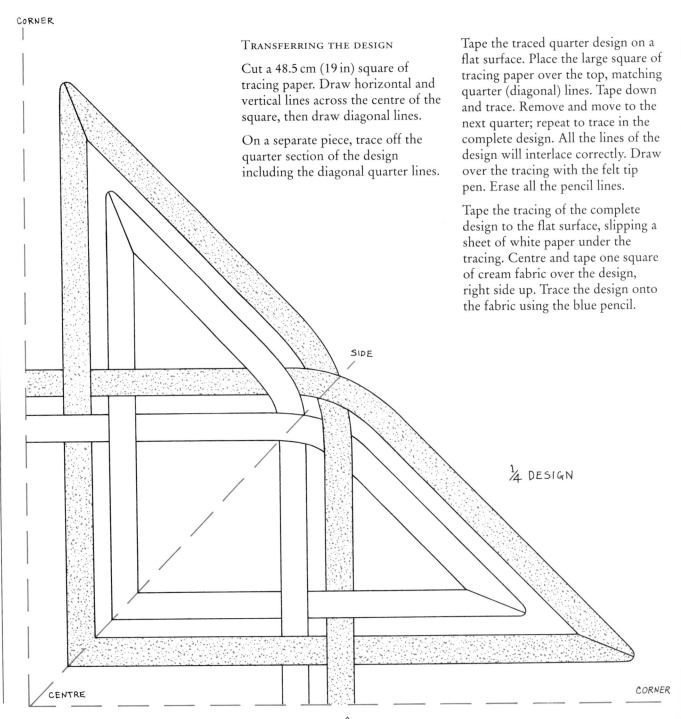

Transferring the design

Cut a 48.5 cm (19 in) square of tracing paper. Draw horizontal and vertical lines across the centre of the square, then draw diagonal lines.

On a separate piece, trace off the quarter section of the design including the diagonal quarter lines.

Tape the traced quarter design on a flat surface. Place the large square of tracing paper over the top, matching quarter (diagonal) lines. Tape down and trace. Remove and move to the next quarter; repeat to trace in the complete design. All the lines of the design will interlace correctly. Draw over the tracing with the felt tip pen. Erase all the pencil lines.

Tape the tracing of the complete design to the flat surface, slipping a sheet of white paper under the tracing. Centre and tape one square of cream fabric over the design, right side up. Trace the design onto the fabric using the blue pencil.

CORNER

CENTRE

SIDE

CORNER

¼ DESIGN

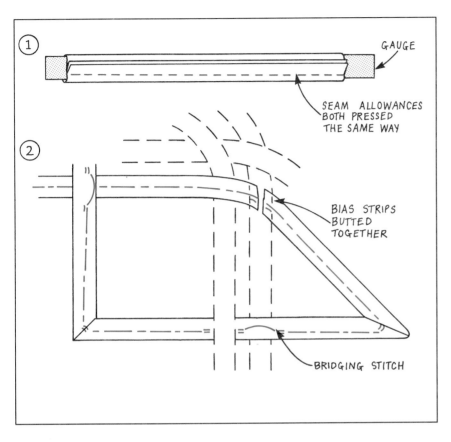

SEAM ALLOWANCES BOTH PRESSED THE SAME WAY

BIAS STRIPS BUTTED TOGETHER

BRIDGING STITCH

GAUGE

gauge (diagram 1). Push the gauge along the tube until the entire length has been pressed. Remove the gauge and gently press again. Wind the pressed strips around a piece of card to keep tidily until required.

WORKING THE APPLIQUÉ

The strips are not joined but the two ends are butted together at cross sections, the join is then covered by another strip going over the top (diagram 2).

Position the strips seam side down along the design lines, beginning under a crossing. Tack in position along centre of strip, making a long stitch over any junction, so that the strips can be woven under and over one another (diagram 2).

Trim the seam allowance and mitre strips carefully on corners (diagram 3). Completely tack a quarter of the design, then sew in place along both edges of the strips with very small hemming stitches and matching threads. Repeat to complete the design.

MAKING UP

Make a sandwich of the appliqué top, wadding and backing fabric as described in the Skill File, page 21. Use cream thread to quilt the cream fabric between the bias strips, outline the inner shapes and around the outer edge of the design. Complete the cushion as described in the Skill File, page 90.

PREPARATION OF BIAS STRIPS

Fold one bias strip in half lengthwise, right side out; machine stitch about 30 cm (12 in) taking a 6 mm (¼ in) seam allowance. Check that the gauge will slip inside the tube snugly altering the position of the stitching if necessary. Stitch all the bias strips in the same way. Trim the seam allowance to 3 mm (⅛ in).

Slip the gauge inside the tube and iron the fabric with the seam allowances both pressed in the same direction along the centre of the

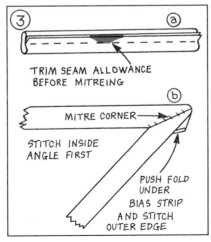

TRIM SEAM ALLOWANCE BEFORE MITREING

MITRE CORNER

STITCH INSIDE ANGLE FIRST

PUSH FOLD UNDER BIAS STRIP AND STITCH OUTER EDGE

CHRISTMAS CUBES

Use exciting, colourful Christmas fabrics to make these cubes, then add more decoration with simple machine appliqué motifs. The blocks could also be made up in patterned fabrics with the appliqué spelling out a child's name.

REQUIREMENTS

30 cm (¼ yd) of six different 115 cm (45 in) wide cotton fabrics (B,C,D,E,F), including a striped design (A)

15 cm (6 in) square of white cotton fabric

Fusible bonding web

1 m (1 yd) of 1.3 cm (½ in) wide ribbon

1 m (1 yd) of 3 mm (⅛ in) wide ribbon

Machine embroidery threads

Matching sewing threads

Six 7.5 cm (3 in) cubes of foam or polyester wadding

Tracing paper

Thin card for template

CUTTING DETAILS

Use the 7.5 cm (3 in) square template on page 52, adding 6 mm (¼ in) seam allowance all around.

Cut 11 squares in fabric A (striped fabric).

Cut 5 squares from fabrics B, C, D, E and F.

FINISHED SIZE

Each block is a 7.5 cm (3 in) cube

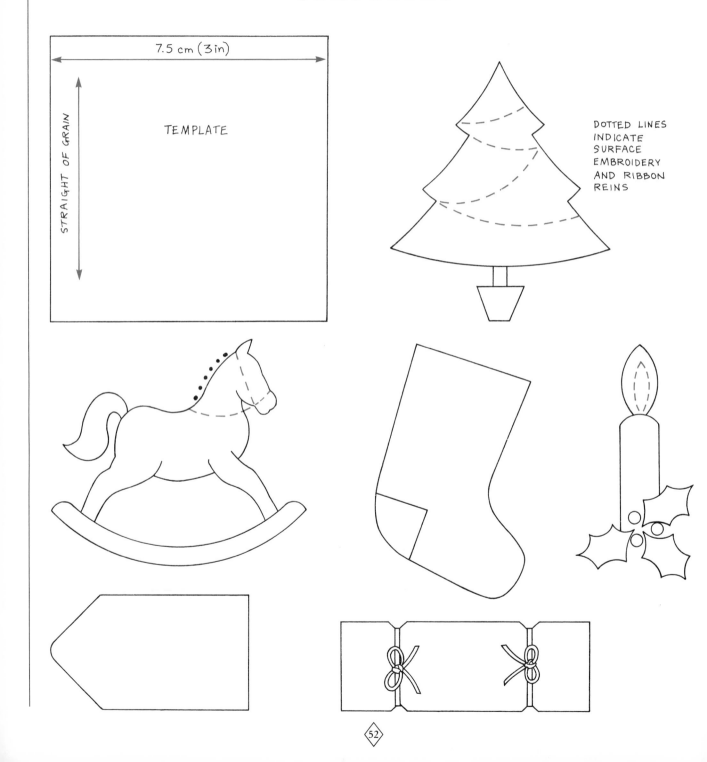

7.5 cm (3 in)

STRAIGHT OF GRAIN

TEMPLATE

DOTTED LINES
INDICATE
SURFACE
EMBROIDERY
AND RIBBON
REINS

WORKING THE APPLIQUÉ

Trace off the motifs onto tracing paper, turn the tracing over and lay on a flat surface. Trace the motifs onto the paper side of the fusible bonding. Cut out each motif, leaving a margin all around each one.

Place these shapes onto the wrong side of the chosen fabrics, paper side up. Iron, then press again over a damp cloth. Allow to cool. Carefully cut out each motif around the outlines.

Peel off the paper and pin the motifs (except for the label) centrally to the right side of the appropriate square. Iron in place; press with a damp cloth.

The 'gift-wrapped' block is made from 6 squares of striped fabric. Cut a 35.5 cm (14 in) length of 1.3 cm (½ in) wide ribbon. Position down the centre of one square; stitch down both edges, leaving

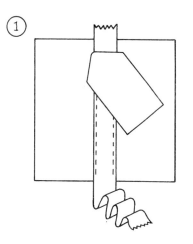

1.3 cm (½ in) free at both ends. Iron the label in place (diagram 1). Embroider names on the label, if liked. Fold the extra ribbon and pin onto the square, so that it will not get caught up in the stitching. Refer to your sewing machine manual for instructions on satin stitch, make a trial square to practise on.

First straight machine stitch, then work a machine satin stitch all around each motif, covering the straight stitching and raw edges and adding extra detail on the candle flame and heel of the stocking.

MAKING UP

Following the configuration shown, make up each cube from six squares

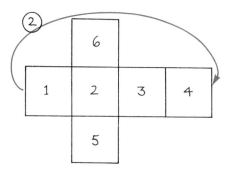

(diagram 2). Use the striped fabric only for the gift cube. Pin and machine (or backstitch by hand) the squares together, as shown in diagram 3. Do NOT stitch into seam allowances.

Stitch side 1 to side 4. Sew the three free sides of square 5 in place to make the base, pinning and stitching each side separately as before.

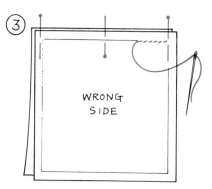

WRONG SIDE

Turn seam allowance on square 6 and the tops of 1, 3 & 4 to the wrong side and tack. Turn each cube right side out. Insert a foam cube or fill with 7.5 cm (3 in) squares of wadding. Ladder stitch around the opening on the right side. On the gift block, take the ribbon round and stitch the ends into the seam.

To decorate, tie ribbon around the gift cube, at right angles to stitched ribbon, into a bow on top. Make bows on the cracker and Christmas stocking and ribbon reins on the horse with the narrow ribbon. Add surface embroidery as liked, e.g. French knots for the horse's mane, beads for the berries on the holly and stitched decorations on the cracker and Christmas tree.

Note: Avoid adding beads and sequins if the blocks are for young children.

CHILD'S PINAFORE

This delightful pinafore features appliqué perse. Motifs cut from the dress fabric are machine stitched around the skirt. The skirt is then gathered onto a simple high bodice which fastens at the back with three buttons. The dress is a simple high bodice style, available in commercial patterns.

REQUIREMENTS

1.20 m (1¼ yd) of 90 cm
  (36 in) wide fine cotton
  lawn or mull
Printed motifs cut from
  dress fabric
Matching sewing threads
Fusible bonding web
Machine embroidery
  thread to match motifs
Three buttons
Sheet of dressmakers'
  pattern paper

CUTTING DETAILS

Use the pattern pieces for the bodice (page 57), adding 1.3 cm (½ in) seam allowance all round, except for hems, where 5 cm (2 in) has been allowed.
Cut 2 front bodices.
Cut 4 back bodices.
Cut 1 skirt front 71 cm (28 in) wide and 38 cm (15 in) long.
Cut 2 skirt backs 38 cm (15 in) square.

FINISHED SIZE

To fit a 3-year-old.

CONSTRUCTION

WORKING THE APPLIQUÉ

Make up two bodice sections (one for lining). Place bodice front and back with right sides facing and stitch together along the shoulder and side seams (diagram 1, overleaf). Press the seams open.

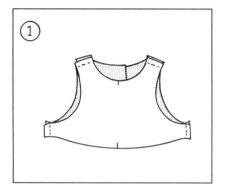

Place skirt front and backs with right sides together; pin and stitch the side seams. Tack and stitch 1.3 cm (½ in) hems along the centre back of the skirt (diagram 2). Press the complete skirt out flat, right side up.

Leaving 1.3 cm (½ in) margins all around, cut out motifs from dress fabrics. Iron fusible bonding to the wrong side of each motif and press with damp cloth. Allow to cool, then cut around each motif. Peel off the protective backing paper.

Arrange the motifs in a pleasing pattern on the skirt and pin in place,

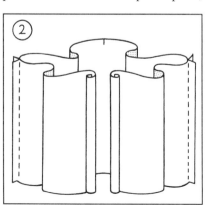

then iron in position using a damp cloth to fix them. Straight machine stitch around each motif, then work a machine satin stitch around each motif over the straight stitching and raw edges using threads to enhance the design.

MAKING UP

Work two rows of gathering stitches around the skirt top. Place one bodice section to the skirt with right sides together, matching centre fronts, side seams and side back skirt hems to large Os on back bodice. Pull up the gathering threads to fit the skirt to the bodice and secure the threads. Tack and stitch together between the rows of gathering (diagram 3).

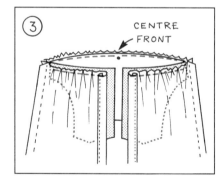

Place the second bodice (the lining) to the wrong side of the skirt with wrong side uppermost; tack and stitch all around. The gathered skirt seam allowance will now be sandwiched between the two bodice sections. Stitch the bodices together down the centre back.

Bring the bodices up and match side

THE DOUBLE BODICE TACKED AROUND NECK AND ARMHOLES

and shoulder seams; tack together round neck and armholes (diagram 4). Cut 4 cm (1½ in) wide bias strips and join together until long enough to bind neck and armholes. Fold in half lengthwise and bind neck and armholes as shown in the Skill File, page 90.

Turn up 5 cm (2 in) hem, tuck under the raw edge and hemstitch. Work three buttonholes on the back and stitch buttons to the opposite side to correspond (diagram 5).

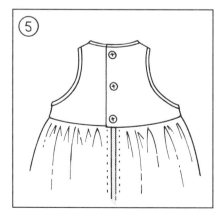

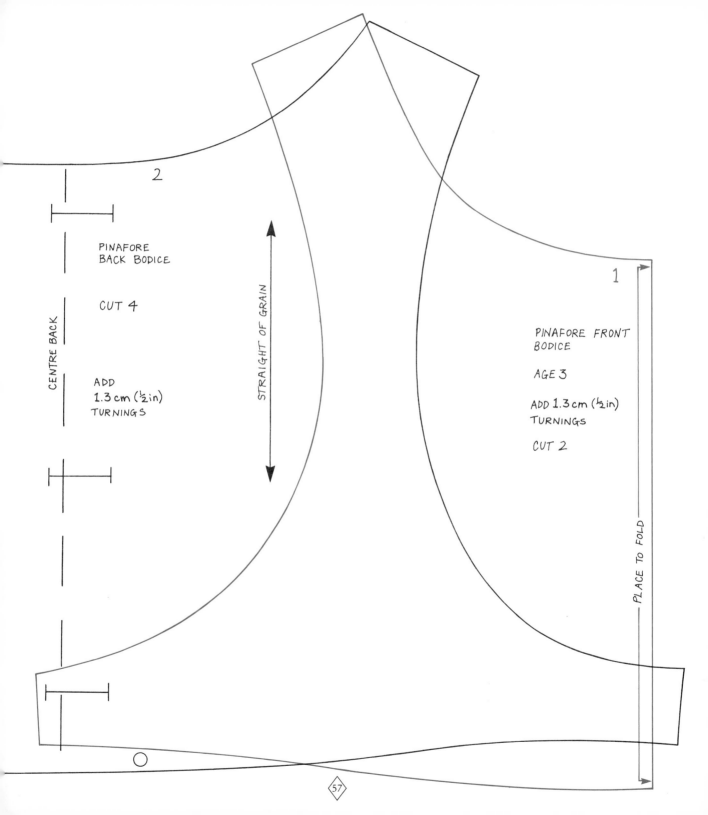

2

PINAFORE
BACK BODICE

CUT 4

CENTRE BACK

ADD
1.3 cm (½in)
TURNINGS

STRAIGHT OF GRAIN

1

PINAFORE FRONT
BODICE

AGE 3

ADD 1.3 cm (½in)
TURNINGS

CUT 2

PLACE TO FOLD

HAWAIIAN-STYLE CUSHION

Hawaiian women were introduced to patchwork by the wives of American missionaries; they then adapted the idea to their own designs to create a form of appliqué. The design is cut from one piece of fabric, using a technique similar to the designs cut from folded paper made by children. The finished result is always quilted in flowing lines following the contour of the appliqué.

REQUIREMENTS

70 cm (¾ yd) of 115 cm
    (45 in) wide mid blue
    cotton fabric for cushion
    front and back
70 cm (¾ yd) of 115 cm
    (45 in) wide white cotton
    fabric for appliqué,
    backing and piping
70 cm (¾ yd) of 115 cm
    (45 in) wide 2 oz wadding
Tracing paper
2.30 m (2½ yd) of piping
    cord
Fine permanent ink black
    felt tip pen
Light blue pencil
46 cm (18 in) square
    cushion pad

CUTTING DETAILS

Wash and iron fabrics.
Blue fabric: cut two 48.5 cm
(19 in) squares.
White fabric: cut one 31.5 cm
(12½ in) square and one 48.5 cm
(19 in) square. Cut remaining
white fabric into 4 cm (1½ in)
wide bias strips (45° from
selvage) and join together to
make a strip approximately
102 cm (40 in) long.

FINISHED SIZE

Cushion is 46 cm (18 in) square

CONSTRUCTION

WORKING THE APPLIQUÉ

Trace the design illustrated on page 61 and cut on design lines. This is ⅛ of the complete motif.

Fold the small white square in half right side in, pressing the folds carefully with an iron. Fold into quarters and press again. Fold again on the diagonal to form a triangle and press (diagrams 1–3, overleaf). Ensure that all the raw edges are laying on top of one another.

Place the pattern on the folded fabric, matching dotted lines to folds. Pin the pattern in place (diagram 4, overleaf). Using very sharp, small scissors cut exactly to the pattern outlines (not along the

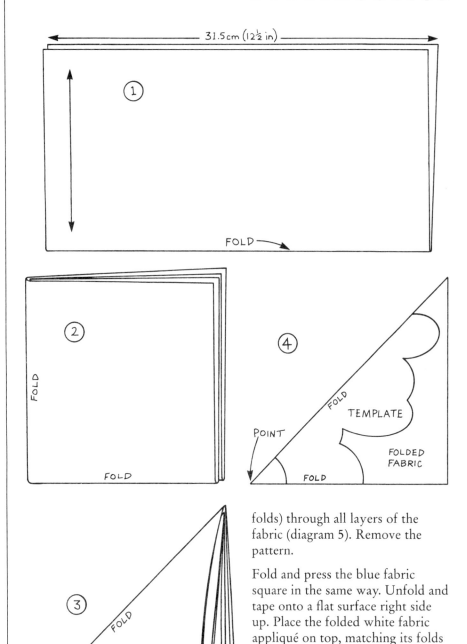

31.5 cm (12½ in)

①

FOLD

②

FOLD

FOLD

④

POINT

FOLD

TEMPLATE

FOLDED
FABRIC

FOLD

③

FOLD

POINT

appliqué to the blue fabric along the radiating lines, leaving 1.3 cm (½ in) free at both ends of each row of tacking. Using small stitches, tack around the design 6 mm (¼ in) in from the edges (diagram 6).

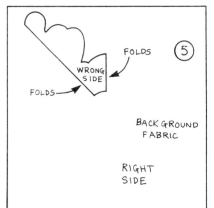

⑤

FOLDS

WRONG
SIDE

FOLDS

BACKGROUND
FABRIC

RIGHT
SIDE

⑥

folds) through all layers of the fabric (diagram 5). Remove the pattern.

Fold and press the blue fabric square in the same way. Unfold and tape onto a flat surface right side up. Place the folded white fabric appliqué on top, matching its folds to the pressed lines on the blue fabric (diagram 5). Carefully open out, matching fold lines. Pin from the centre out, then tack the

Using white thread, work small neat, tight hemming stitches around the design, turning under the raw edges by stroking them with the needle, behind the thumb and against the tacking stitches. This will give a 3 mm (⅛ in) turning (diagram 4, page 19).

Traditionally in Hawaiian appliqué curves are not clipped. The seam allowances are turned in and stitched as smoothly as possible, this will result in a rounded flowing design. Where necessary reinforce inner curves with tiny, oversewing stitches.

Cut the blue fabric away from the back of the white appliqué, leaving 6 mm (¼ in) turnings (diagram 1, page 17). Press the finished appliqué on the wrong side.

MAKING UP

Prepare the quilting sandwich, see the Skill File, page 21 and quilt in flowing lines, 1.3 cm (½ in) apart, over the complete article, following the contours of the design.

Add piping around the quilted cushion front and stitch to the cushion back. Insert a cushion pad following the Skill File, page 90.

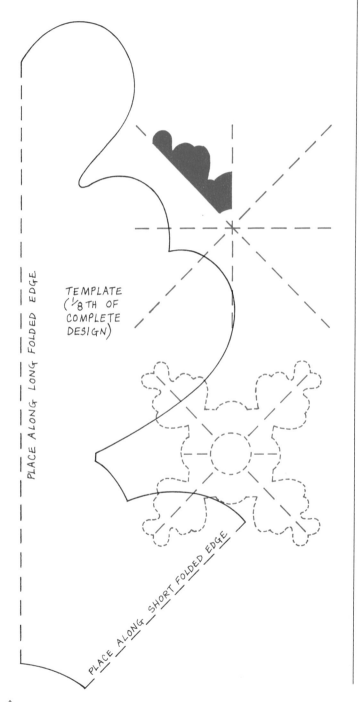

PLACE ALONG LONG FOLDED EDGE

TEMPLATE
(⅛TH OF
COMPLETE
DESIGN)

PLACE ALONG SHORT FOLDED EDGE

ORGANDIE TABLECLOTH

This small delicate tablecloth looks elegant draped over a small occasional table. The pink scalloped border is edged with machine satin stitch, while the tulip and leaves are applied on one corner by hand using punch stitch.

REQUIREMENTS

1.20 m (1¼ yd) of 115 cm (45 in) wide cotton organdie
1.20 m (1¼ yd) of 115 cm (45 in) wide fine pink cotton fabric
20 cm (8 in) square of fine white cotton fabric
Machine embroidery cotton
White sewing thread
White stranded cotton
Tracing paper
Fine permanent black ink felt tip pen
Light blue pencil

CUTTING DETAILS

Organdie: Cut one 94 cm (37 in) square
Pink fabric: Cut four strips 94 × 10 cm (37 × 4 in). Cut one tulip adding 2.5 cm (1 in) all around.
White fabric: Cut leaves, adding 2.5 cm (1 in) all around each one. Spray starch pink fabric strips and iron dry.

FINISHED SIZE

Tablecloth is 91.5 cm (36 in) square

CONSTRUCTION

WORKING THE APPLIQUÉ

Make a 46 cm (18 in) long scallop template by tracing the section given on page 65 three times and adding a corner section (diagram 1, overleaf). Glue the tracing to thin card and cut out. The straight end is the centre of the border.

Mark the centres of the pink strips. Place the template on the right side of the fabric, matching centre lines and leaving a 1.3 cm (½ in) seam allowance on the long straight edge. Draw around the template with blue pencil. Turn the template over

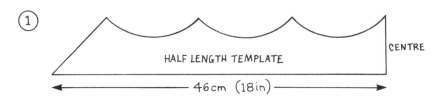

① HALF LENGTH TEMPLATE

CENTRE

← 46cm (18in) →

and matching centres again, trace the other half. Repeat on all the border strips.

Place 2 strips with right sides together; pin and stitch together along the diagonal lines. Trim the seam allowance to 6 mm (¼ in) and press open. Join all the strips together in the same way to form a frame (diagram 2).

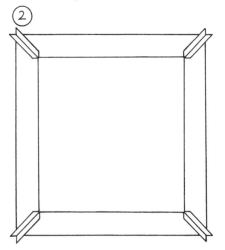

②

Place the pink fabric frame over the organdie with right sides together. Tack and stitch around the outer edges, taking a 1.3 cm (½ in) seam allowance (the stitching line marked on the right side of the strips will be visible through the organdie). Press the seam allowance open. This stitching line will become the fold line on the edge of the cloth.

Turn to the right side. Lay the work on a flat surface and gently ease the fabric frame into position. Fold along the stitching line and tack around the outer and inner edges and 1.3 cm (½ in) inside the drawn scalloped edges (diagram 3).

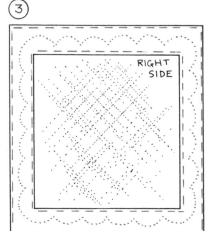

③

RIGHT SIDE

Straight machine stitch through both layers along the scalloped edge. Remove the inner line of tacking and cut the pink fabric only, close to the stitching. Work a machine satin stitch over the straight stitching and raw edges.

Trace the tulip design in the corner of the cloth with a blue pencil.

Tack in place on the right side of the fabric. Using white sewing thread and a chenille needle work

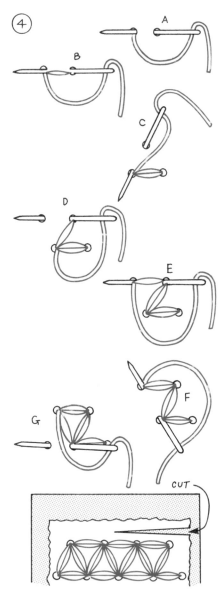

④ A

B

C

D

E

F

G

CUT

punch stitch (diagram 4) all around the design lines. Trim the fabric close to the embroidery. Prepare and stitch the leaves in the same manner. Embroider the stem and leaf veins in stem stitch.

TEMPLATES

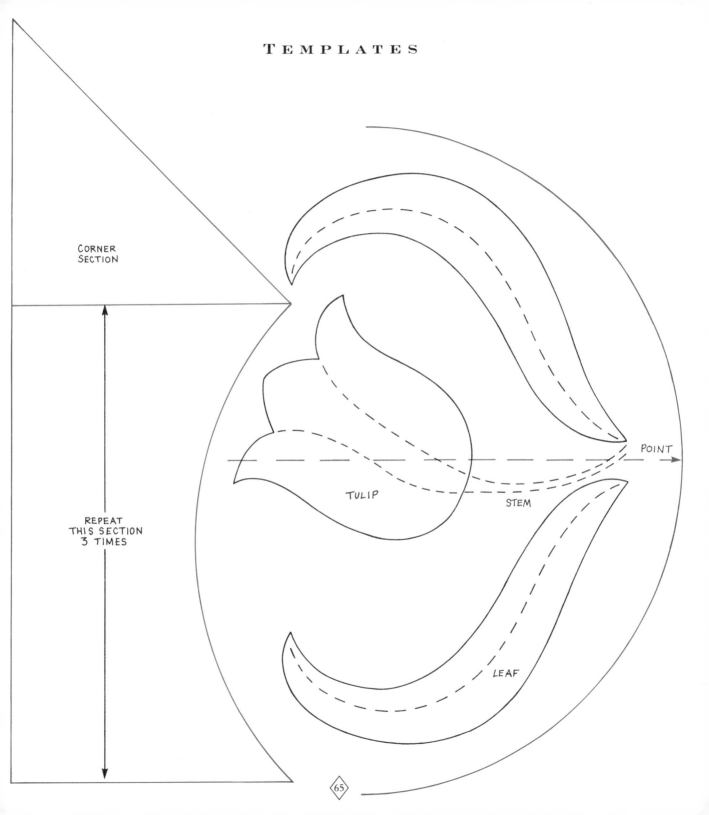

CORNER SECTION

REPEAT THIS SECTION 3 TIMES

TULIP

STEM

LEAF

POINT

NEEDLEWORK BAG

Perfect for storing your sewing or knitting projects, this useful bag has a hand stitched Dresden Plate block consisting of eighteen petals and an appliqué centre worked on each side.

REQUIREMENTS

Two 33 cm (13 in) squares of cotton fabric for background

Twelve 20 cm (8 in) squares of different patterned fabrics

Two 10 cm (4 in) squares of plain cotton fabric for centre

Card for template

Matching sewing threads

One 15 cm (6 in) square of tracing paper

Sheet of fine glasspaper

FINISHED SIZE

The bag measures approximately 58 × 43 cm (23 × 17 in)

CUTTING DETAILS

Make a petal template from card or plastic. Make a centre circle from card (see page 68).

Using a compass, set the radius to 12.5 cm (5 in) and draw a circle on the tracing paper. From the same centre point, draw a smaller circle with a radius of 2.5 cm (1 in). Fold the tracing paper into quarters through the centre and cut out both circles. This is the stitching guide.

Smooth patterned fabric onto glasspaper right side down. Mark round petal template on wrong side of fabric, add 6 mm (¼ in) seam allowance. Cut 6 shapes from each of the patterned fabrics – 36 petals in all.

Plain fabric: Mark and cut 2 circles, adding 6 mm (¼ in) seam allowance all around.

CONSTRUCTION

WORKING THE APPLIQUÉ

Fold the backing fabric in half and then in quarters; press. Unfold and mark the creased lines with coloured tacking stitches. Place the stitching guide onto the background fabric, matching fold lines to quarter lines on background fabric; pin in place. Tack around the outer edges of the guide on the background fabric, keeping very close to the edge. Mark the centre circle in the same way (diagram 1, overleaf). Remove the guide.

Place the petals in sequence so that the six colours are each repeated three times.

On the outer edges of the petals, needlemark the fold lines as in the Skill File, page 18. On each of the 18 petals, turn this seam allowance to the wrong side and tack.

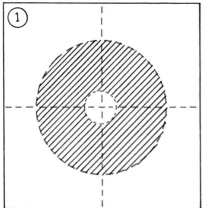

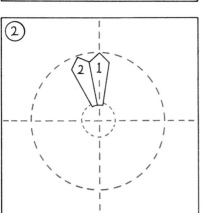

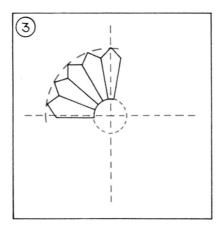

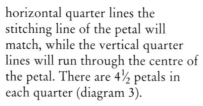

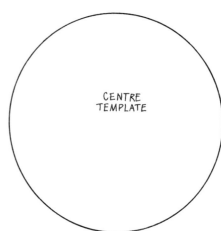

CENTRE
TEMPLATE

horizontal quarter lines the stitching line of the petal will match, while the vertical quarter lines will run through the centre of the petal. There are 4½ petals in each quarter (diagram 3).

Make sure that the petals are correctly placed on these quarter marks. Stitch the 18 petals in place, turning the outer long edge of the last one and slipstitching it over the first petal. Slipstitch all around the outer edge of the design.

Work a gathering thread 3 mm (⅛ in) in from the cut edge of the centre circle, place the card circle on the wrong side of the fabric, pull up the gathering thread and press (as in Martha Washington's Wreath, page 29). Carefully remove the card. Pin a circle of wadding a little smaller than the template to the wrong side. Place in the centre of the design and stitch in place.

Cut out and make up the second appliqué piece in the same way.

Place the first petal on the background fabric, right side up, with the vertical quarter line running through the middle and the petal point touching the guide line (diagram 2). Pin in place. For petal 2 and all the remaining petals, lay right side down over the preceding shape. Sew in place along the stitching line with small running stitches through all three layers. Open the petal out, so that the point touches the guide line. Press each petal as you work. On the

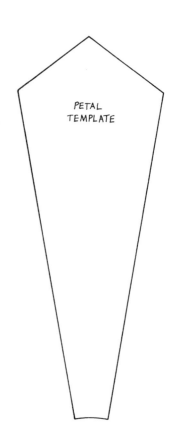

PETAL
TEMPLATE

Bag

REQUIREMENTS

1.90 cm (2 yd) of 115 cm
  (45 in) wide cotton fabric
70 cm (¾ yd) of 90 cm
  (36 in) wide 2 oz wadding
Matching sewing threads
Two 40 cm (16 in) long
  pieces of dowel for
  handles

CUTTING DETAILS

Cut 2 gusset strips 104 × 7.5 cm (41 × 3 in)

Cut 2 bag lining pieces 56 × 43 cm (22 × 17 in)

Make up 2 × 30 cm (12 in) appliqué blocks (page 67)

Cut 2 strips 33 × 7.5 cm (13 × 3 in) for base and 4 strips 38 × 7.5 cm (15 × 3 in) for sides

Cut 2 top sections 43 × 20 cm (17 × 8 in) – the 'U' shapes are cut later

Cut a 5 cm (2 in) wide bias strip, approximately 370 cm (145 in) long (join as necessary).

MAKING UP

Pin and stitch the base strip to the base of the appliqué block. Stitch on the side strips, then the top strip.

With the bag lining wrong side up, place the wadding on top, then bag front; pin and tack. Quilt around the plate and outer edge of block.

Make up the back and the front of the bag the same way.

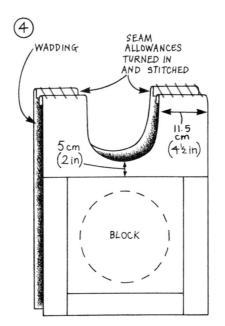

Cut a 'U' shape from the top of the bag front and back (diagram 4). Fold in 1.3 cm (½ in) seam allowance on both sides of front and lining, trim wadding and oversew together.

Fold the bias strip in half lengthwise and stitch around the 'U' shapes on the right side, through all layers. Trim the seam allowance to 6 mm (¼ in), roll the folded edge to the wrong side and slipstitch in place.

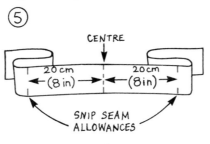

Place the gusset strips with right sides together; stitch short ends. Turn to the right side. Tack together along both the long sides. Mark the centre of the gusset on both sides. Measure 20 cm (8 in) on either side of the centre and snip the seam allowance almost up to the stitching lines (diagram 5).

Note: The bag is constructed with seams on the outside.

Pin and stitch gusset to the centre base of the bag front, to the corners, then up the side of the bag. Attach the gusset to the bag back in the same way (diagram 6).

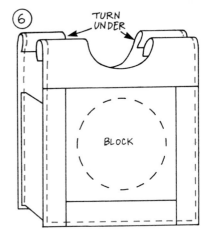

Turn 5 cm (2 in) to the inside of the bag on either side of the 'U' shape, tack together at the sides.

Bind all the raw edges and seams of the bag on back and front, as in the Skill File, page 90, place the dowelling under the folded tops; slipstitch the folded edges to the bag lining.

PINK CARNATION PICTURE

An elegant 17th century embroidery motif is the basis of this hand stitched design. The petals and calyxes are built up on one another to give a layered and more naturalistic look to the picture. The finished result has been professionally framed with a double mount.

FINISHED SIZE

The picture is approximately 30 cm (12 in) square

CONSTRUCTION

TRANSFERRING THE DESIGN

Trace the complete design onto tracing paper using a black felt tip pen (page 72). Tape the tracing to a flat surface. Centre the background fabric, right side up over the tracing. Trace the complete design onto the fabric with a blue pencil.

WORKING THE APPLIQUÉ

Draw up templates for the petals, calyxes and leaves, extending them under succeeding petals (page 72). The extensions are indicated by the dotted lines on the design, except for the large pink. For this flower follow the exploded diagram.

Reversing the templates, mark around each shape on the wrong side of the appropriate fabric. Cut out, adding 3 mm (⅛ in) allowance all around.

Needlemark around the stitching line on the wrong side of the fabric as each shape is to be stitched in position, see the Skill File, page 18.

Cut 2.5 cm (1 in) wide bias strips for the stems. The stems are sewn in

STEM 3

CALYX
8

1

5

3

9

7

2

6

4

STEM 4

6

1

STEM
1

2

1

2

STEM 2

3

1

5

2

4

6

5

3

2

1

4

7

8

9

72

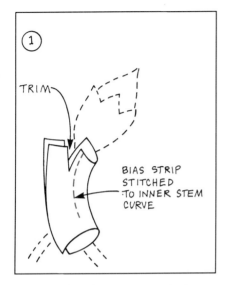

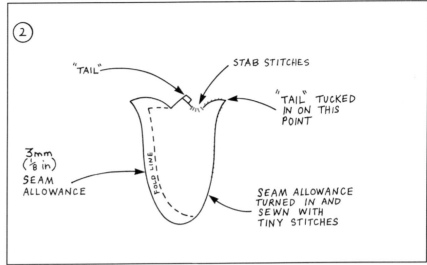

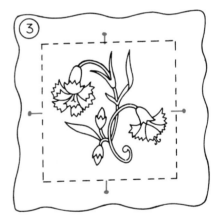

position first, beginning with the upper bud stem (diagram 1). Stitch stems in place in the same way as for Martha Washington's Wreath, page 29, following the numbered order on the design. Always complete each stem, covering cut ends with the next applied shape. Tease the end of stem 4 into a little knob as shown in the photograph.

Needlemark and tack the petals and calyxes as each one is to be applied. Follow the numbered order of stitching. With these shapes it will be necessary to snip down into the points. Always begin stitching on the longer smooth edge. On the outer points of the calyxes and petals, stroke under the tails, see the Skill File, page 20. Stitch down to the inner points and stitch around the weak point with a semicircle of small stab stitches over the raw edge (diagram 2).

Stitch the leaves in place over the stems, tucking the points in and strengthening the inner curves.

Embroider stamens on both carnations using stem stitch and French knots on the large carnation using 1 strand of embroidery cotton, see page 92.

MAKING UP

To prepare the work for framing place the wadding over the backing card, then add the appliqué. Smooth the work out from the centre and pin into the card edge in the centre of each side (diagram 3). Still smoothing out from the centre insert more pins into the edges of the card all around. Fold the excess fabric to the back of the card and fix in place with masking tape. Check the design is central and remove the pins. Frame as desired.

SCROLL DESIGN PLACE MAT

Reverse appliqué has been used to achieve the distinctive effect on these place mats. In this type of appliqué the top fabric is cut and hand stitched in a pattern exposing the contrast fabric underneath.

REQUIREMENTS FOR EACH MAT

2 pieces of fine cotton fabric
  46 × 30 cm (18 × 12 in)
2 pieces of fine cotton fabric
  in a contrast colour 11.5
  × 30 cm (4½ × 12 in)
DMC perlé thread No 5 to
  match both fabrics
HB pencil
Fine black permanent ink
  felt tip pen
White or blue pencil
Tracing paper
Spray starch

FINISHED SIZE

Each mat measures 43 × 28 cm
(17 × 11 in)

CONSTRUCTION

TRANSFERRING THE DESIGN

Wash, spray starch and iron the fabrics.

The section of the design (page 77) is repeated three times along each short edge. To draw the complete design, trace the section as shown, including the horizontal centre line and parallel lines on either side. Cut this drawing from the tracing paper.

On a large sheet of tracing paper draw two parallel lines 28 cm (11 in) long and 7 cm (2¾ in) apart. Draw a horizontal line 14 cm (5½ in) down for the centre of the mat.

①

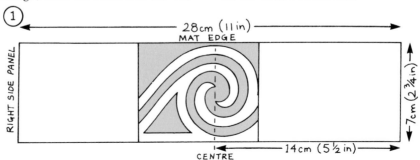

28cm (11 in)
MAT EDGE
RIGHT SIDE PANEL
7cm (2¾ in)
14cm (5½ in)
CENTRE

Place the tracing of the design under this grid matching vertical and centre lines. Trace the design (diagram 1, previous page) then reposition and trace the design to left and right of the central design, matching the vertical and scroll design, extending at the right to complete the side panel. Draw over the panel with black felt tip pen and erase the pencil lines. Add another parallel vertical line 1.3 cm ($\frac{1}{2}$ in) at the top. This is the complete design for the right-hand side of the mat (diagram 2).

The left-hand side is a mirror image of the right, so simply turn the design over and make a second tracing using the black felt tip pen.

When the drawing is complete, draw in the broken blue lines to mark where the top fabric will be cut. This is particularly useful as the design when drawn on the fabric can be very confusing – it is all too easy to cut between the wrong lines. On the right side, allowing for 1.3 cm ($\frac{1}{2}$ in) turnings, mark

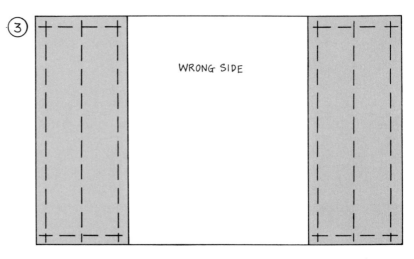

stitching lines all around the mat. Tack a line horizontally across centre of mat.

Tape the traced designs onto a flat surface, slipping a sheet of white paper underneath. Tape the fabric over the top, matching up centres and the straight edge of the pattern lines to the stitching lines. Trace the design onto the fabric with a white or blue pencil and mark in the broken cutting lines with a different coloured pencil.

WORKING THE APPLIQUÉ

Tack the two strips of contrasting fabric onto the wrong side of the top fabric across the two short ends (diagram 3). Turn to the right side and stitch through the two layers with small tacking stitches in the middle of those areas of the design which will not be cut.

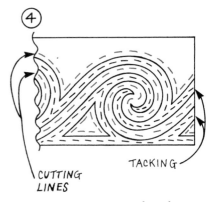

Note: It is important that the stitching is in the middle and is tightly and accurately sewn (diagram 4).

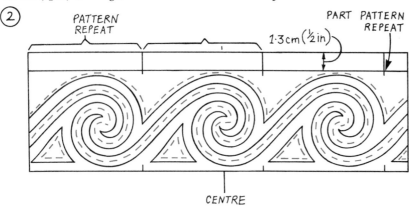

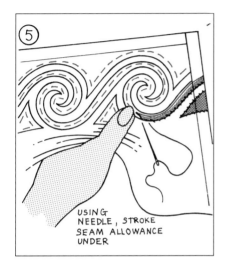

USING NEEDLE, STROKE SEAM ALLOWANCE UNDER

contrast fabric appears both within the scroll design and on the outer edges of the mat.

MAKING UP

Lay the completed appliqué right side up on a flat surface. Place the second fabric piece on top with right sides together aligning the edges carefully. Pin and tack the layers together. Back stitch by hand or machine stitch all around, following the marked lines and leaving a 15 cm (6 in) opening centrally along one long edge.

Trim the seam allowances leaving 6 mm (¼ in) on the backing and 8 mm (⅜ in) on the mat front, thus layering them. Trim across corners and turn to right side. Turn in the edges of the opening and slipstitch together.

On the right side redraw the parallel lines on either side of the appliqué design. Using perlé thread, sew through all layers with back stitch, keeping the top stitches about 6 mm (¼ in) apart, reversing the colours, to give the effect of a line of beads.

Beginning at the right-hand side, cut along the broken lines through the top fabric only for approximately 5 cm (2 in). Holding the work in the hand, use the needle to stroke the raw edges under (diagram 5). Work against the pressure of the thumb and the small tacking stitches. This will give a seam allowance of approximately 3 mm (⅛ in). Use matching thread and small, tight hemming stitches. Only cut short lengths through the design at any time.

It may be necessary to snip seam allowances on curves and on points, but do not cut as far as the fold lines. Snip just enough to release the tension on the fabric so the seam allowance can be rolled under. Where it is necessary to snip into corners, work a group of small oversewing stitches to strengthen the edge. Gradually the outer edge of the top fabric is cut away and the

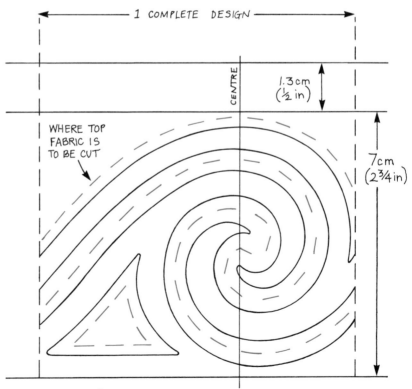

1 COMPLETE DESIGN

CENTRE

1.3 cm (½ in)

7 cm (2¾ in)

WHERE TOP FABRIC IS TO BE CUT

CHRISTMAS HANGING

The much loved poinsettia, Christmas rose and holly are worked in machine appliqué with the addition of some 3D pieces to provide interest. The three roundels are suspended from an elegant fabric bow.

REQUIREMENTS

For the pictures:
Three 15 cm (6 in) diameter
    Flexi hoops
50 cm (½ yd) of 115 cm
    (45 in) wide fabric for
    background and frame
    backing
30 cm (¼ yd) of 115 cm
    (45 in) wide cotton fabric
    in red, green and white
5 cm (2 in) of yellow fabric
30 cm (¼ yd) of 115 cm
    (45 in) wide 2 oz wadding
Machine embroidery
    threads
Yellow stranded cotton
Matching sewing thread

New tissue paper
Spray starch
1 m (1 yd) of 3 mm (⅛ in)
    wide ribbon to match bow

For the bow:
30 cm (¼ yd) of 115 cm
    (45 in) wide fabric
30 cm (¼ yd) of 82 cm
    (32 in) wide iron-on
    interfacing
Matching sewing thread

FINISHED SIZE

Each design is a 15 cm
(6 in) circle

CUTTING DETAILS

Cut three 23 cm (9 in) squares from background fabric, one for each hoop. Spray starch and iron dry.

CONSTRUCTION

Trace the designs (pages 82–3) excluding the templates onto tissue paper.

Centre each traced design onto the right side of each background square; pin in place. Trace tack (take short tacking stitches through tissue paper and background fabric) just inside the design outline (diagram 1, overleaf). Score the paper along the tacking lines with a needle and gently pull the paper away.

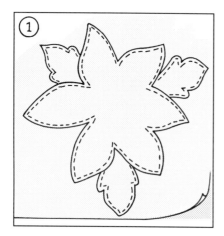

Poinsettia

Cut three rectangles from green fabric large enough to cover the shaded area (see page 82) and to extend under the red bract to the dotted lines. Pin in position on the right side of the background. Turn to wrong side. Machine stitch just outside the tacked line. Turn to right side and cut close to the

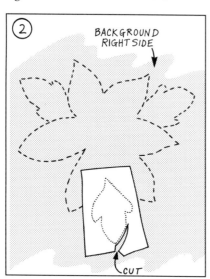

machine stitched lines (diagram 2). Cut red fabric large enough to cover the red bract area; pin to the right side and stitch as before.

Using machine embroidery threads, work a machine satin stitch covering the straight stitching and raw edges, around first the green bracts then the red bracts. Stitch in the vein details in straight stitch.

To make the 3D bracts cut two 15 cm (6 in) squares of red fabric and one 15 cm (6 in) square of wadding. Cut a bract template (page 82) from thin card.

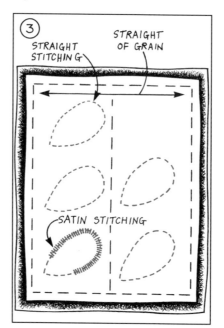

Place the template on one red square across the bias and draw around five times (diagram 3), leaving at least 1.3 cm (½ in) between each one. Lay the second

piece of red fabric, wrong side up on a flat surface, place the wadding over the top and then the marked red fabric. Tack the sandwich together as shown.

Straight machine stitch around the shapes through all layers, then machine satin stitch over the straight stitching. Cut out close to the satin stitching, with small, sharp scissors, taking care not to cut any stitches. As the bract has been sewn on the bias it will curl slightly as it is sewn in position. Arrange these five bracts in the centre of the appliquéd bract, radiating from the centre dot, pin in position then straight machine stitch along the middle, simulating veins through all layers.

Embroider yellow flowers in the centre with French knots (page 92).

The Christmas Rose and Holly Spray
are worked using the same preparation method.

Christmas Rose
Appliqué the leaf to the background fabric.

Use white fabric for the five 3D petals. Mark the top fabric using the petal template. Make the sandwich of fabrics and wadding; tack and stitch as before. Arrange the petals radiating from the leaf centre dot, pin in position, then straight machine stitch using pale green thread, referring to the shading marked on the petal template, through all layers.

Make the flower centre from yellow fabric (see 'Heart of Leaves' project, page 37) and embroider French knots around it.

Holly

Machine satin stitch the stem, widening the stitches towards the base. Appliqué two holly leaves to the background fabric as before, then make up three individual padded leaves using the leaf template, as described above. Attach to the background fabric where indicated by dotted lines with straight machine stitches along the centre of the leaves, to simulate veins, through all layers.

Make and attach the holly berries as described in the 'Heart of Leaves' project.

Place a Flexi frame over each completed appliqué and draw a circle. Sew a line of gathering stitches 1.3 cm (½ in) outside the marked circle using strong thread, trim fabric to 1.3 cm (½ in) outside the gathering line. Place the inner frame in position on the wrong side of the work; pull up the gathering thread tightly and tie off. Lace from side to side (diagram 4).

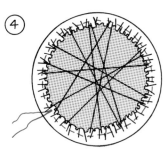

Mark around the inner frame on the wrong side of the backing fabric; cut out adding 6 mm (¼ in) seam allowance. Turn seam allowance in and stitch over the back of the work to neaten.

Bow

Cut two 11.5 cm (4½ in) wide strips across the fabric width. Cut off the selvages and join into one strip approximately 224 cm (88 in) long.

Cut 5 cm (2 in) wide strips of iron-on interfacing to the same length as the fabric. Iron centrally to the wrong side of the fabric strip, joining strips by overlapping.

Fold the strip lengthwise, right sides together. Stitch long edges with 6 mm (¼ in) seam allowance, leaving 15 cm (6 in) opening in the centre. Centre the seam and press open. Stitch across the ends and trim the corners (diagram 5). Turn to the

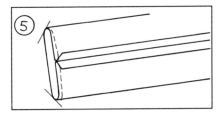

right side; gently shape the corners and slipstitch the opening together, press.

To make the bow, fold as shown in diagrams 6 and 7, securing the folds with stitches behind the 'knot'. Tie the roundels at regular intervals along the narrow ribbon. Make a hanging loop at the top of the

ribbon, and stitch the ribbon to the back of the bow. Arrange the tails of the bow behind the pictures.

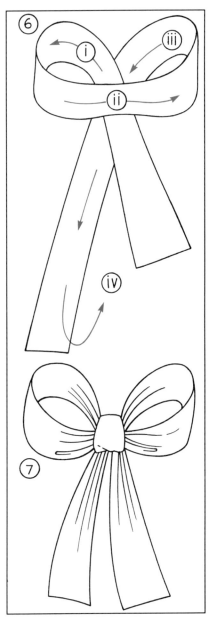

TEMPLATES

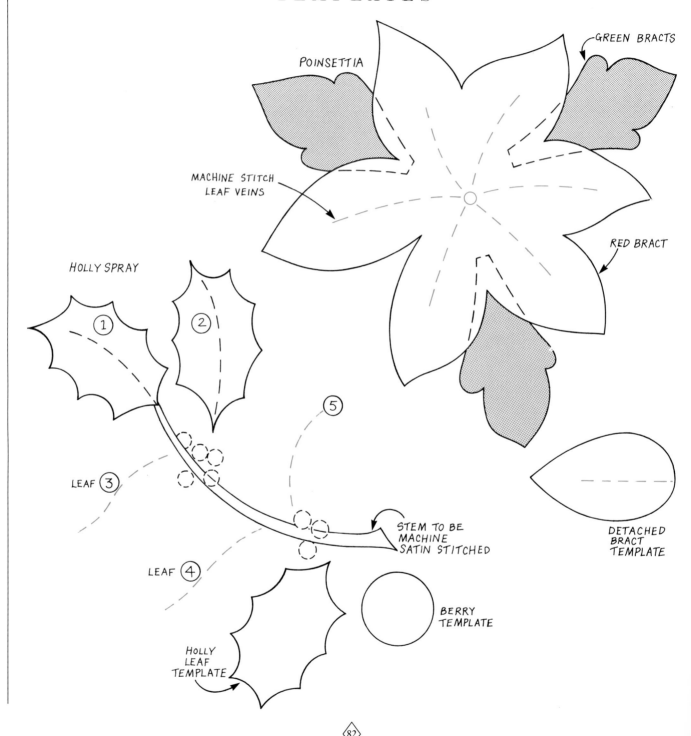

GREEN BRACTS

POINSETTIA

MACHINE STITCH LEAF VEINS

RED BRACT

HOLLY SPRAY

① ② ⑤

LEAF ③

LEAF ④

STEM TO BE MACHINE SATIN STITCHED

DETACHED BRACT TEMPLATE

HOLLY LEAF TEMPLATE

BERRY TEMPLATE

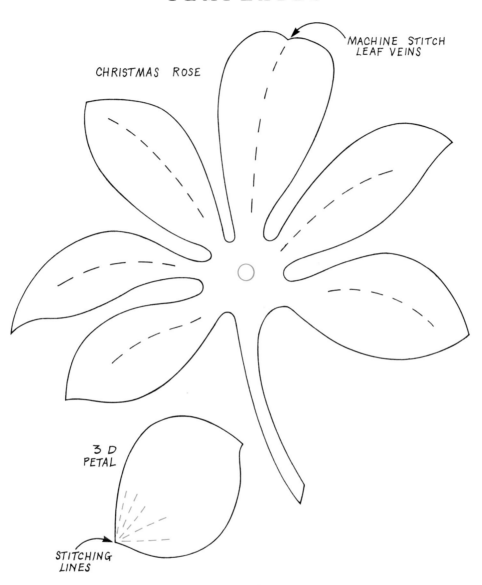

CHRISTMAS ROSE

MACHINE STITCH
LEAF VEINS

3 D
PETAL

STITCHING
LINES

Sweet Pea Panel

This shadow appliqué panel features the much loved sweet pea, framed within an oval and decorated with an elegant bow. Shadow work enables pretty, intricate shapes to be stitched with ease. The various shapes are cut from fabric, covered by a semi-sheer fabric and sewn with a running stitch. The panel is then quilted to intensify the colours and add texture.

Requirements

50 cm (½ yd) of 115 cm (45 in) wide white cotton fabric

50 cm (½ yd) of 115 cm (45 in) wide pale grey cotton fabric

30 cm (¼ yd) of 115 cm (45 in) wide pale pink cotton fabric*

30 cm (¼ yd) of 115 cm (45 in) wide medium pink cotton fabric*

50 cm (½ yd) of 115 cm (45 in) wide white mull or voile for top

50 cm (½ yd) of 115 cm (45 in) wide 2 oz wadding

15 cm (6 in) squares of cotton fabric in the following colours*: light mauve, medium mauve, dark mauve, vibrant pink, light green, medium green and dark green

DMC perlé thread No 5 in green and mauve

Pale green stranded cotton

Sewing threads to match colours of fabric as they appear through mull

Spray starch

Glue stick

Light blue pencil

Tracing paper

Fine black permanent ink felt tip pen

2 strips of wood 28 × 2 cm (11 × ¾ in)

* Check the coloured fabrics as they appear through the mull. The colours will intensify once the fabrics are stitched together, but change any that do not give the desired effect. Colours which have any black in them can look dull.

CUTTING DETAILS

Wash all fabrics, spray starch coloured fabrics and iron them all carefully.
White fabric: Cut two pieces 43 × 33 cm (17 × 13 in), one for the foundation and one to back the design.
Mull: Cut one piece 43 × 33 cm (17 × 13 in).
Pale grey fabric: Cut one piece 43 × 33 cm (17 × 13 in).

FINISHED SIZE

The panel measures 38 × 28 cm (15 × 11 in)

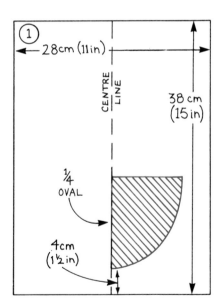

WORKING THE APPLIQUÉ

Draw the outer rectangular frame on tracing paper 38 × 28 cm (15 × 11 in). Mark the centre vertical line.

Make a separate tracing of the quarter oval frame (page 89). Place this tracing under the rectangular frame, matching the vertical centre line, 4 cm (1½ in) up from the base line (diagram 1); mark round the outer edge. Repeat, to mark in the remaining three sections. The oval frame is not centred lengthwise.

Trace the spray of sweet peas (page 88) within the oval and position the bow over the top, as shown (diagram 2). Draw over the whole design with black felt tip pen. Erase all pencil lines.

Lay the white foundation fabric over the drawing and tape in position. Using the blue pencil, trace the oval, marking the vertical centres, bouquet and diagonal lines which are initial guide lines for

quilting. Remove carefully and keep flat.

Place the pale grey fabric over the drawing, tape in position, trace oval, again marking the centres, bow and inner frame line. Carefully cut out the oval.

Tape the foundation fabric to a flat surface, lay the pale grey fabric over the top, matching up centre lines. Keep flat.

Trace the various sweet pea petals, calyxes, leaves and bow directly on to the various starched fabrics, using the blue pencil. Cut out without adding seam allowances, but extending the shapes where applicable, so they can be overlapped by an adjacent shape, avoiding the need to butt two cut edges together (diagram 3).

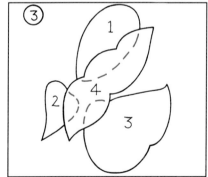

If it is difficult to see the design lines through the darker fabrics, then make the necessary templates from thin card and mark round these onto the fabrics. The small leaflets, stems and tendrils will be treated in a different way.

Touch the wrong side of each coloured shape with the glue stick and place in the correct sequence. Place the mull over the complete design; pin, then tack always starting from the centre. Tack central horizontal and vertical lines, then diagonally, then around the oval and all around the outer edge. Tack any flower shapes that have been missed.

Stitch around the flowers, leaves and bow with very small running stitches through all three layers, just inside the cut edges. Match the sewing thread to the colour as it appears through the mull.

Using the pale green sewing thread, stitch two parallel lines about 3 mm (⅛ in) apart for the stems and outline the two leaflets. Stitch around the oval just inside the cut edge, then two more rows, one on each side of the original stitching line about 3 mm (⅛ in) apart. Remove the tacking, except from around the outer edges.

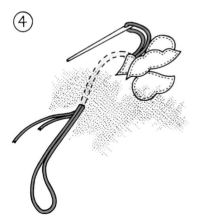

④

Using a tapestry needle, thread two strands of green perlé through the stems (diagram 4). Cut the threads leaving 6 mm (¼ in) free at both ends. Smooth along each stem, taking care not to cut the mull trim off the excess perlé cotton, pushing the ends of the threads into the channels with the tapestry needle. Fill the leaflets by drawing the perlé cotton through twice.

Insert mauve perlé cotton threads into the double channels around the oval. It will be necessary to fill both channels in two operations: top left to bottom left, then top right to bottom right, leaving 1.3 cm (½ in) tails at each end. When all four half channels have been filled, smooth the channels along the cords and trim away the excess, as before.

Lay the stitched panel over the drawing again and remark the quilting guide lines and tendrils on the top fabric.

Tape backing fabric wrong side uppermost on a flat surface. Lay the wadding on top, then the stitched panel. Pin in the centre. Smooth out to the edges and insert more pins. Tack as before, adding more horizontal and vertical lines to hold the sandwich securely together.

Using white thread, quilt around the flower spray and inside the oval frame, then quilt the diagonal background diamonds. Using green sewing threads, quilt veins on the large and medium leaves. Using pale grey thread, quilt around the outer

edge of the oval, round the bow and two lines of quilting 3 mm (⅛ in) apart around the frame line. Mauve perlé threads can be inserted between these rows if required.

Use one strand of green embroidery cotton to embroider tendrils with stem stitch, see page 93. Trim the edges of the quilted panel leaving 1.3 cm (½ in) seam allowance.

Making up

From the pale grey fabric cut 4 cm (1½ in) wide bias strips. Cover sufficient piping cord and pipe around the panel, see Skill File, page 90.

From the grey fabric cut two strips 28 × 10 cm (11 × 4 in). Fold each piece in half lengthwise with right sides together; stitch, taking 1.3 cm (½ in) seam allowance. Centre the seam and press open. Stitch across one end (diagram 5). Turn right side

⑤
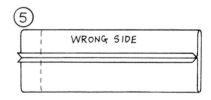
WRONG SIDE

out. Turn in the remaining end and slipstitch. Slipstitch the strips to the back at top and base, below and above the piping.

Drill a hole 1.3 cm (½ in) in from each end of one of the wood strips, to take the hanging cord. Slip the strip through the top sleeve. Insert second strip in the bottom sleeve.

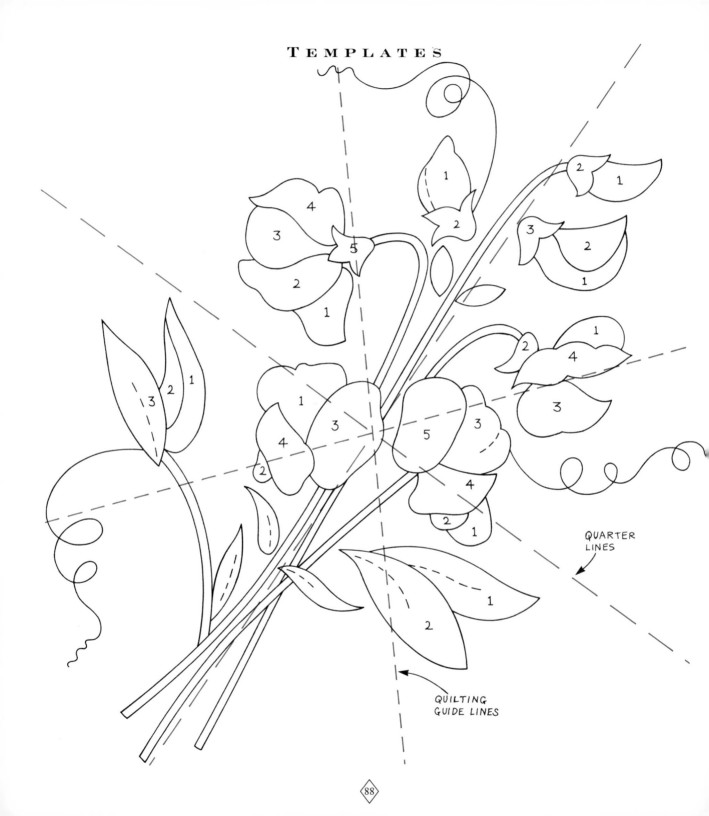

QUARTER
LINES

QUILTING
GUIDE LINES

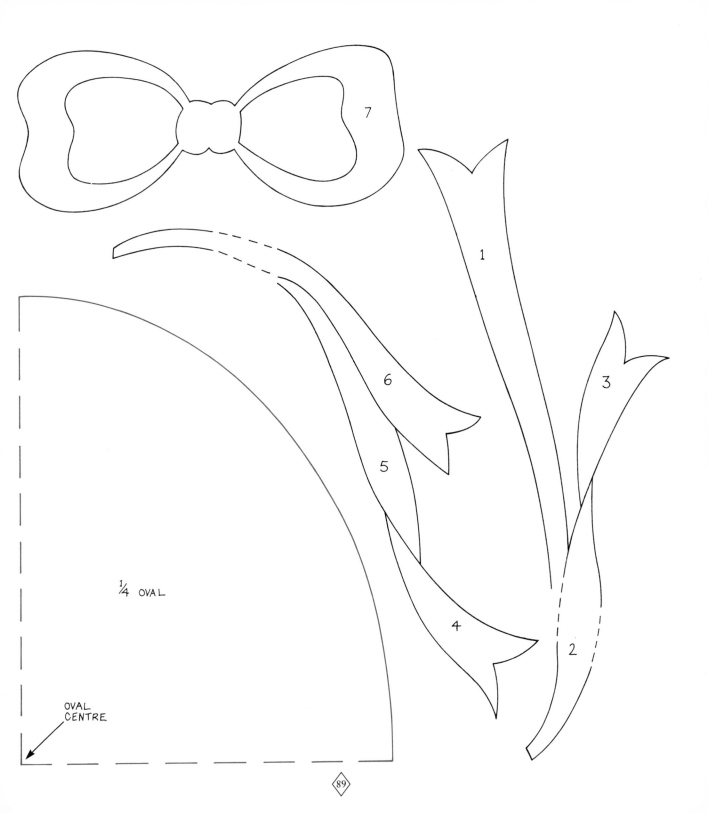

7

1

3

6

5

¼ OVAL

4

2

OVAL
CENTRE

FINISHING

To pipe a quilt or panel

Boil the piping cord to shrink it. Cut sufficient bias strips of fabric 4 cm (1½ in) wide to go around the article, joining as necessary. Fold the fabric strip around the piping cord, right side out (diagram 1); tack close to the cord along the length.

Tack the covered cord to the right side of the appliqué through the top and wadding only, clipping the seam allowance on corners (diagram 2).

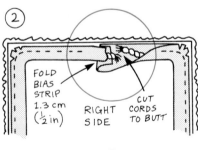

FOLD BIAS STRIP 1.3 cm (½ in)   RIGHT SIDE   CUT CORDS TO BUTT

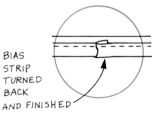

BIAS STRIP TURNED BACK AND FINISHED

To join the piping, cut and butt cord ends together; turn under one fabric end and overlap the opposite raw end (diagram 2).

Stitch all around the edges close to the piping cord. Turn the raw edges in bringing the covered cord to the edge of the appliqué.

Fold the backing seam allowances in and slipstitch in place under the covered cord (diagram 3), covering the stitching.

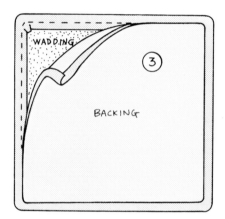

WADDING

③

BACKING

To pipe a cushion

Work in the same way as before, but stitch the piping through top, wadding and backing fabrics. Place the cushion back over the piped cushion front with right sides together. Stitch together around the edges, close to the cord, but leave an opening along the bottom edge. Trim across corners and turn to the right side. Insert a cushion pad the same size as the cover; turn in the edges of the opening and slipstitch together.

Binding the edges

Cut a bias strip six times the desired finished width. Fold the strip in half lengthwise. The double thickness binding gives a full rounded edge which will wear well. Stitch in place through all layers – the binding, appliqué top, wadding and backing.

To mitre the corners, pin the bias strip in place. Stitch along the seam line up to the corner, but not into the allowance. Finish off the thread securely. Insert a pin at 45° to the corner (diagram 4a), fold the strip up over the pin and fold back (4b),

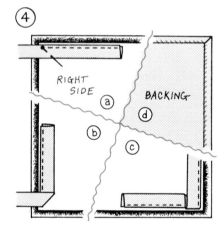

④

RIGHT SIDE   ⓐ   BACKING   ⓓ

ⓑ   ⓒ

then take it down the second edge (4c); pin, stitch to the next corner and proceed as before.

Turn the folded edge of bias strip over onto the backing and slipstitch in place. At the corners, press the first fold in firmly, turn the folded edge of the bias strip over onto the second edge, forming a neat mitre on the back (diagram 4d).

CARE AND CONSERVATION

Caring for textiles

The main enemies of textiles are sunlight, which fades and rots the fibres, and dust and dirt.

The following information on care and conservation, storage and cleaning has particular reference to quilted appliqué. Other sound, securely stitched appliqué can be treated in a like manner *but* shake the article *very gently*. Silk and other fragile appliquéd textiles should not be hung but laid flat, upside down over a dry towel and *patted very gently*.

It cannot be overstated that valuable, exquisite textiles should only be cleaned and restored by professional conservationists.

Generally it is good practice to give appliquéd articles, including quilts, an airing from time to time by hanging them on a clothes line, padded with a sheet, with the right side inside to protect them from the light. Choose a fine, fresh, breezy day and shake the quilt from time to time to dislodge the dust. Leave for about an hour. This airing will help to fluff up the wadding. If it is not possible to hang a quilt outside, set the vacuum cleaner on minimum suction, cover the nozzle with a firmly secured piece of muslin and clean gently and carefully.

Storage

Do not use plastic bags or plastic sheeting to store textiles as they attract dirt and can encourage the growth of moulds.

Rolling: Rolling is the best method of storing a quilt. Use a cardboard tube wrapped in wadding. Lay the quilt wrong side up, cover with acid-free tissue paper and roll around the tube. The right side of the quilt will be on the outside. Wrap more tissue paper around it and slide the roll into a cotton fabric bag. This makes a rather unwieldy package, but is the method that should be used for silk quilts as folding can crack the fabric.

Folding: Where it is necessary to fold a quilt, avoid making sharp creases by laying acid-free tissue paper over the whole quilt and adding wadding where it will be folded. Fold carefully and store in a large cotton fabric bag or fold in a sheet. Do not place other items on top as this will increase the pressure on the folds.

Cleaning

It is a good idea to have silk and wool quilts professionally dry cleaned.

Most cotton quilts can be washed but check colour fastness. Quilts with cotton wadding are very heavy when wet, so help would be required.

Cotton quilts with polyester wadding are usually better washed by hand. Choose a fine, breezy day when they can be hung out in the garden. Wash large items in the bath in cool water using good quality soap flakes. Squeeze as much of the water out of the quilt as possible. Do not wring, but the quilt can be given a short spin if it will fit in the washing machine. Hang the quilt, right side in on a line padded with a sheet. Shake the quilt frequently during the drying time.

Quilts can be steamed; pass a steam iron over the quilt without letting the weight of the iron down on the quilt. The heat of the iron would flatten the polyester wadding and it would not recover.

Cleaning antique quilts

Always take expert advice before cleaning an old and valued quilt.

Old worn quilts and unfinished pieces of patchwork and appliqué are often offered for sale. If the price is right for you, they can be conserved by covering with fine silk net or the appliqué could be reapplied to a new background fabric. Old, valuable or loved fragments of printed fabrics and embroidery can also be applied to a new background to conserve them.

GLOSSARY

Appliqué Sewing fabric shapes onto a background fabric by hand or machine.

Appliqué perse Cutting out printed motifs and applying them to a background fabric.

Bias strip A strip cut diagonally 45° across the warp and weft threads of a piece of fabric.

Blind hemming Small tight stitches, which are almost invisible, used for hand appliqué, see page 20.

Block A complete unit of an appliqué or patchwork design.

Bonding web A fusible bonding adhesive with a paper backing.

Card/cardboard Lightweight illustration board used for templates.

Cartridge paper/drawing paper Smooth surfaced paper used for sketching and designing.

Celtic appliqué Bias strips of fabric applied in interwoven and curved designs.

Construction seam allowance When making up articles 1.3 cm (½ in) seam allowances need to be added for strength.

French knots Bring the thread out of the fabric and hold it taut. Twist the needle round the thread two or three times and tighten the twists.

Still holding the thread taut, turn the needle round and insert it into the fabric very close to the point where it emerged. Pull the thread through the fabric.

Grain line A line following the warp threads parallel to the selvage edge.

Hawaiian appliqué Appliqué design cut from one complete piece of fabric and contour quilted.

Marked line Line drawn round a template marking the stitching line.

Needlemarking A method of marking the fold line (the stitching line) on fabric shapes which are to be appliquéd.

Organdie Very fine cotton fabric with inherent stiffness.

Patchwork The construction of a complete textile using interlocking shapes.

Piping cord/filler cord Strong cord available in various diameters which is encased in bias-cut strips to make a decorative edge.

Polystyrene/Styrofoam A lightweight board suitable for pinning fabric shapes onto.

Punch stitch Hand embroidered three-sided stitch which can be used for appliqué, see page 64.

Quilting The sewing together of a sandwich consisting of top,

wadding and backing, using running stitches.

Running stitch This basic stitch is quick and simple to do. Work from right to left, taking the needle in and out of the fabric at regular intervals. The stitches and intervals between should be a similar size.

Sashing or setting strips/dividers Lattice strips of fabric which are used to divide or outline the blocks when assembling them into a complete top.

Satin stitch Work each stitch across the shape, returning beneath the fabric close to the point where the needle emerged. Keep the stitches close together and of even tension.

Shadow appliqué Coloured fabric shapes placed on a foundation fabric then covered by a semi-sheer fabric and stitched in place.

Slipstitch Slide the needle along the fold of the fabric for a short distance then take up a small amount of the backing fabric and take the needle back into the fold. The stitches should be almost invisible.

Stab stitch Keep the needle at right-angles to the work, take the needle through all layers to the back of the work, then push the needle back again at right angles.

Stem stitch This stitch produces a neat raised line. Work stem stitch along the lines of the design. Insert the needle into the fabric at a slight angle along the marked line, keeping the working thread to the right of the needle. All the stitches should be the same size.

Tack/tacking/baste/basting Large temporary running stitch used to hold pieces of fabric together. Only take up a few fabric threads between each stitch.

Template The exact pattern from which the component parts of a design are cut.

Wadding/batting The middle, soft and fluffy layer of the quilt sandwich, giving warmth and loft.

ACKNOWLEDGEMENTS

Photographs on pages 10 and 13 reproduced by permission of The American Museum in Bath, Britain.

Picture framing by Ian Hunter.

Celtic appliqué cushion stitched by Mary Atkins.

INDEX